buy·OLOGY

DOUBLEDAY

new york   london   toronto
sydney   auckland

buy·OLOGY

TRUTH *and*

LIES *about*

why we BUY

martin
LINDSTROM

Book design by Terry Karydes

Library of Congress Cataloging-in-Publication Data
Lindstrom, Martin, 1970–
    Buyology : truth and lies about why we buy / by Martin Lindstrom.
        p. cm.
    Includes bibliographical references and index.
    (hc : alk. paper) 1. Neuromarketing. 2. Consumer behavior.
3. Shopping—Psychological aspects. 4. Marketing—Psychological
aspects. I. Title.
    HF5415.12615.L56 2008
    658.8'34—dc22

                                    2008006057

ISBN 978-0-385-52388-2

PRINTED IN THE UNITED STATES OF AMERICA

10   9   8   7   6   5   4   3   2   1

First Edition

CONTENTS

It was a brisk September night. I was unprepared for the weather that day, wearing only a tan cashmere sweater underneath my sports jacket. I was still cold from the walk from my hotel to the pier as I boarded the crowded cruise ship on which I was going to meet Martin Lindstrom for the first time. He had spoken that day at a food service conference held by the Gottlieb Duttweiler Institute, the venerable Swiss think tank, and David Bosshart, the conference organizer, was eager for us to meet. I had never heard of Martin before. We moved in different circles. However, I had seen *BRANDchild*, Martin's latest book, in the JFK airport bookstore before I flew into Zurich.

Anyone seeing Martin from twenty feet away might mistake him for someone's fourteen-year-old son, being dragged reluctantly to meeting after meeting with his father's overweight graying business associates. The second impression is that somehow this slight blond creature has just stepped into the spotlight—you wait for the light to fade, but it doesn't.

Like a Pre-Raphaelite painting there is a glow that emanates from Martin as if he was destined to be on stage. No, not as a matinee idol, but as some god waif. The man exudes virtue. Close up, he is even more startling. I've never met anyone with such wise eyes set in such a youthful face. The touch of gray and the slightly crooked teeth give him a unique visual signature. If he weren't a business and branding guru, you might ask him for an autographed picture or offer him a sweater.

I don't think we exchanged more than ten words that night seven years ago. But it was the start of a personal and professional friendship that has stretched across five continents. From Sydney to Copenhagen, from Tokyo to New York, we conspire to make our paths cross. Laughter, discussion, mutual council—it has been a unique pleasure. Martin spends three hundred nights a year on the road. I don't have it that bad, but after a certain point you stop counting the strange pillows and discarded flight coupons and just enter into the comradeship of road warriors.

Martin watches, listens, and processes. The bio on his Web site says he started his advertising career at age twelve. I find that less interesting than the fact that at about the same age his parents pulled him out of school, hopped on a sailboat and went around the world. I know that at age twelve I couldn't have lived on a ten-meter boat for two years with my parents. Martin says he still gets seasick and chooses to live in Sydney, which is about as far away from his native Denmark as you can get.

In the world of learned discourse what is fun is finding yourself sharing opinions with people whose pathway to that point of view has been different from yours. It's both a form of validation and a reality check. In my career as an anthropologist of shopping, I haven't always seen eye to eye with advertisers and marketers. For one, I have a fundamental distrust of the twentieth-century fascination with branding; I don't own shirts with alligators or polo players on them and I rip the labels off the outside of my jeans. In fact, I think companies should pay *me* for the privilege of putting their logo on my chest, not the other way around. So it's a bit strange for me to find myself in the same pulpit with someone who is passionate about branding and believes that advertising is actually a virtuous endeavor, not just a necessary evil. What we share is the belief that the tools for understanding why we do what we do, whether it's in shops, hotels, airports, or online, need to be reinvented.

Through the end of the twentieth century merchants and marketers had two ways of examining the efficacy of their efforts. First was tracking sales. What are people buying and what can we ascertain from their purchase patterns? I call it the view from the cash register. The problem is that it validates your victories and losses without really explaining why they're happening. So they bought Jif peanut butter, even though Skippy was on sale.

The second tool was the traditional market research process of asking questions. We can stop people as they stroll down the concourse of the mall, we can call them up on the phone, we can invite them to a focus group or ask them to join an Internet panel. I know from long experience that what people say they do and what they actually do are different. It does not mean that those two tools are not functional, just that they are limited. Just as advertising and branding still work—but they don't work the same way they used to.

The problem was that we are better at collecting data than

doing anything with it. In the nineties the offices of many
market researchers were stacked with printouts, whether on
television ratings and viewing, scanner data from sales research, or the results of thousands of phone interviews. We
learned that soccer moms between the ages of 28 and 32,
driving late model minivans and living in small towns, prefer
Jif two to one over Skippy. What do we do with the information? As one cynical friend suggested, we are looking to get
beyond the so what, big deal, and what-can-I-do-with-this
information test.

Science and marketing have historically had a love-hate relationship. In the 1950s academicians ventured out of their
ivory towers and began collaborating with advertising agencies. Vance Packard's seminal book *The Hidden Persuaders* describes that golden era that lasted less than a decade. Making
moms feel good about feeding their children Jell-O, or decon-
structing why a sexy sports car in the front of the Ford deal-
ership sold Plain Jane sedans off the back lot. Much of it was
simple and logical. Applying it was easy with three major television channels and roughly a dozen popular magazines. The
relationship started unraveling when stuff just went wrong. In
the fifties, in spite of the best brains and a very healthy marketing budget, the Edsel flopped. Thirty years later New Coke
tanked.

For the past three decades the science in market research
was more about higher math than psychology. Statistical relevance, sample size, standard deviation, Z-tests and T-tests and
so on. The absolutes of math are somehow safer. I like to
think that the modern market researcher is in the business of
making his clients better gamblers by seeking to cut the odds.
Call it a cross between scientist and crystal ball reader: some-

one fast enough to get it right and with enough gift of gab to tell a believable story.

In this volume, Martin, who has spent the past ten years developing new research tools, steps off into neuromarketing. This book is about the new confluence of medical knowledge and technology and marketing, where we add the ability to scan the brain as a way of understanding brain stimulations. What part of the brain reacts to the Coca-Cola logo? How do we understand what part of sex sells?

I guarantee you, it's an enjoyable and informative ride. From fishing villages in Japan to locked corporate board-rooms in Paris to a medical laboratory in Oxford, England, Martin has a treasure chest of fascinating insights to impart and stories to tell. And whatever your feelings about brands and branding—or whether you have any feelings on the sub-ject at all—he'll keep you wanting more.

Will we be able to watch sexual stimulus migrate to differ-ent parts of the brain as procreation and pleasure get further unhooked? Stand back, Michael Crichton—this isn't the sci-ence fiction of time machines or nano-technology run amok. It is Martin Lindstrom and he's got another great book.

buy·OLOGY

Let's face it, we're all consumers. Whether we're buying a cell phone, a Swiss antiwrinkle cream, or a Coca-Cola, shopping is a huge part of our everyday lives. Which is why, each and every day, all of us are bombarded with dozens, if not hundreds, of messages from marketers and advertisers. TV commercials. Highway billboards. Internet banner ads. Strip mall storefronts. Brands and information about brands are coming at us constantly, in full speed and from all directions. With all the endless advertising we're exposed to every day, how can we be expected to remember any of it? What determines which information makes it into our consciousness, and what ends up in our brains' industrial dump of instantly forgettable Huggies ads and other equally unmemorable encounters of the consumer kind?

Here, I can't help but be reminded of one of my numerous hotel visits. When I walk into a hotel room in a strange city, I immediately toss my room key or card somewhere, and a millisecond later I've forgotten where I put it. The data just vanishes from my brain's hard drive. Why? Because, whether I'm aware of it or not, my brain is simultaneously processing all other kinds of information—what city and time zone I'm in, how long until my next appointment, when I last ate something—and with the limited capacity of our short-term memories, the location of my room key just doesn't make the cut.

Point is, our brains are constantly busy collecting and filtering information. Some bits of information will make it into long-term storage—in other words, memory—but most will become extraneous clutter, dispensed into oblivion. The process is unconscious and instantaneous, but it is going on every second of every minute of every day.

The question is one I've been asked over and over again: Why did I bother to write a book about neuromarketing? After all, I run several businesses, I constantly fly all over the globe advising top executives—heck, I'm home only sixty days out of the year. So why did I take time out of my already time-starved schedule to launch the most extensive study of its kind ever conducted? Because, in my work advising companies on how to build better and lasting brands, I'd discovered that most brands out there today are the product equivalent of room keys. I realized that, to clumsily paraphrase my countryman Hamlet, something was rotten in the state of advertising. Too many products were tripping up, floundering, or barely even making it out of the starting gate. Traditional research methods weren't working. As a branding advisor, this nagged at me to the point of obsession. I wanted to find out why consumers were drawn to a particular brand of clothing, a certain make of car, or a particular type of shaving cream, shampoo, or chocolate bar. The answer lay, I realized, somewhere in the brain. And I believed that if I could uncover it, it would not only help sculpt the future of advertising, it would also revolutionize the way all of us think and behave as consumers.

Yet here's the irony: as consumers, we can't ask ourselves these questions, because most of the time, we don't know the answers. If you asked me whether I placed my room key on the bed, the sideboard, in the bathroom, or underneath the TV remote control, consciously, at least, I wouldn't have the foggiest idea. Same goes for why I bought that iPod Nano, a Casio watch, a Starbucks Chai Latte, or a pair of Diesel jeans. No idea. I just did.

But if marketers could uncover what is going on in our brains that makes us choose one brand over another—what information passes through our brain's filter and what information doesn't—well that would be key to truly building brands of the future. Which is why I embarked on what would turn out to be a three-year-long, multimillion-dollar journey into the worlds of consumers, brands, and science.

As you'll read, I soon came to see that neuromarketing, an intriguing marriage of marketing and science, was the window into the human mind that we've long been waiting for, that neuromarketing is the key to unlocking what I call our Buyology—the subconscious thoughts, feelings, and desires that drive the purchasing decisions we make each and every day of our lives.

I'll admit, the notion of a science that can peer into the human mind gives a lot of people the willies. When most of us hear "brain scan," our imaginations slither into paranoia. It feels like the ultimate intrusion, a giant and sinister Peeping Tom, a pair of X-ray glasses peering into our innermost thoughts and feelings.

An organization known as Commercial Alert, which has petitioned Congress to put an end to neuromarketing, claims that brain-scanning exists to "subjugate the mind and use it for commercial gain." What happens, the organization asked once in a letter to Emory University president James Wagner (Emory's neuroscience wing has been termed "the epicenter of the neuromarketing world"), if a neuroscientist who's an expert in addiction uses his knowledge to "induce product cravings through the use of product-related schemes"? Could it even, the organization asks in a petition sent to the U.S. Senate, be used as political propaganda "potentially leading to new totalitarian regimes, civil strife, wars, genocide and countless deaths"?[1]

While I have enormous respect for Commercial Alert and its opinions, I strongly believe they are unjustified. Of course, as with any newborn technology, neuromarketing brings with it the potential for abuse, and with this comes an ethical responsibility. I take this responsibility extremely seriously, because at the end of the day, I'm a consumer, too, and the last thing I'd want to do is help companies manipulate us or control our minds.

But I don't believe neuromarketing is the insidious instrument of corrupt governments or crooked advertisers. I believe it is simply a tool, like a hammer. Yes—in the wrong hands a hammer can be used to bludgeon someone over the head, but that is not its purpose, and it doesn't mean that hammers should be banned, or seized, or embargoed. The same is true for neuromarketing. It is simply an instrument used to help us decode what we as consumers are already thinking about when we're confronted with a product or a brand—and sometimes even to help us uncover the underhanded methods marketers use to seduce and betray us without our even know-ing it. It isn't my intention to help companies use brain-scanning to control consumers' minds, or to turn us into robots. Sometime, in the faraway distant future, there may be people who use this tool in the wrong way. But my hope is the huge majority will wield this same instrument for good: to better understand ourselves—our wants, our drives, and our motivations—and use that knowledge for benevolent, and practical, purposes. (And if you ask me, they'd be fools not to.)

My belief? That by better understanding our own seem-ingly irrational behavior—whether it's why we buy a designer shirt or how we assess a job candidate—we actually gain *more* control, not less. Because the more we know about why we fall prey to the tricks and tactics of advertisers, the better we can defend ourselves against them. And the more companies know about our subconscious needs and desires, the more useful, meaningful products they will bring to the market. Af-ter all, don't marketers want to provide products that we fall in love with? Stuff that engages us emotionally, and that en-hances our lives? Seen in this light, brain-scanning, used ethi-cally, will end up benefiting us all. Imagine more products that earn more money and satisfy consumers at the same time. That's a nice combo.

Until today, the only way companies have been able to un-derstand what consumers want has been by observing or ask-ing them directly. Not anymore. Imagine neuromarketing as one of the three overlapping circles of a Venn diagram. In-vented in 1881, the Venn diagram was the creation of one John Venn, an English logician and philosopher from a no-nonsense Evangelical family. Typically used in a branch of mathematics known as set theory, the Venn diagram shows all the possible relationships among various different sets of abstract objects. In other words, if one of the circles represented, say, men, while the other represented dark hair, and the third, mustaches, the overlapping region in the center would represent dark-haired men with mustaches.

But if you think of two circles in a Venn diagram as representing the two branches of traditional marketing research—quantitative and qualitative—it's time to make room for the new kid on the block: neuromarketing. And in that overlapping region of these three circles lies the future of marketing: the key to truly and completely understanding the thoughts, feelings, motivations, needs, and desires of consumers, of all of us.

Of course, neuromarketing isn't the answer to everything. As a young science, it's limited by our still-incomplete understanding of the human brain. But the good news is that understanding of how our unconscious minds drive our behavior is increasing; today, some of the top researchers around the globe are making major inroads into this fascinating science. At the end of the day, I see this book—based on the largest neuromarketing study of its kind—as my own contribution to this growing body of knowledge. (Some of my findings may be questioned, and I welcome what I believe will result in an important dialogue). Though nothing in science can ever be considered the final word, I believe *Buyology* is the beginning of a radical and intriguing exploration of why we buy. A contribution that, if I've achieved my goal, overturns many of the myths, assumptions, and beliefs that all of us have long held about what piques our interest in a product and what drives us away. So I hope you enjoy it, learn from it, and come away from it with a better understanding of our Buyology—the multitude of subconscious forces that motivate us to buy.

1

A RUSH OF BLOOD

TO THE HEAD

*The Largest Neuromarketing
Study Ever Conducted*

NOT SURPRISINGLY, THE
smokers were on edge, fidgety, not sure what to expect.

Barely noticing the rain and overcast skies, they clumped together outside the medical building in London, England, that houses the Centre for NeuroImaging Sciences. Some were self-described social smokers—a cigarette in the morning, a second snuck in during lunch hour, maybe half-a-dozen more if they went out carousing with their friends at night. Others confessed to being longtime two-pack-a-day addicts. All of them pledged their allegiance to a single brand, whether it was Marlboros or Camels. Under the rules of the study, they knew they wouldn't be allowed to smoke for the next four hours, so they were busy stockpiling as much tar and nicotine inside their systems as they could. In between drags, they swapped lighters, matches, smoke rings, apprehensions: *Will this hurt? George Orwell would love this. Do you think the machine will be able to read my mind?*

Inside the building, the setting was, as befits a medical laboratory, antiseptic, no-nonsense, and soothingly soulless—all cool white corridors and flannel gray doors. As the study got under way I took a perch behind a wide glass window inside a cockpit-like control booth among a cluster of desks, digital equipment, three enormous computers, and a bunch of white-smocked researchers. I was looking over a room dominated by an fMRI (functional Magnetic Resonance Imaging) scanner, an enormous, $4 million machine that looks like a giant sculpted doughnut, albeit one with a very long, very hard tongue. As the most advanced brain-scanning technique available today, fMRI measures the magnetic properties of hemoglobin, the components in red blood cells that carry oxygen around the body. In other words, fMRI measures the amount of oxygenated blood throughout the brain and can pinpoint an area as small as one millimeter (that's 0.03937 of an inch). You see, when a brain is operating on a specific task, it demands more fuel—mainly oxygen and glucose. So the harder a region of the brain is working, the greater its fuel consumption, and the greater the flow of oxygenated blood will be to that site. So during fMRI, when a portion of the brain is in use, that region will light up like a red-hot flare. By tracking this activation, neuroscientists can determine what specific areas in the brain are working at any given time.

Neuroscientists traditionally use this 32-ton, SUV-sized instrument to diagnose tumors, strokes, joint injuries, and other medical conditions that frustrate the abilities of X-rays and CT scans. Neuropsychiatrists have found fMRI useful in shedding light on certain hard-to-treat psychiatric conditions, including psychosis, sociopathy, and bipolar illness. But those smokers puffing and chatting and pacing in the waiting room weren't ill or in any kind of distress. Along with a similar sample of smokers in the United States, they were carefully chosen participants in a groundbreaking neuromarketing study who were helping me get to the bottom—or the brain—of a mystery that had been confounding health professionals, cigarette companies, and smokers and nonsmokers alike for decades.

For a long time, I'd noticed how the prominently placed health warnings on cigarette boxes seemed to have bizarrely little, if any, effect on smokers. *Smoking causes fatal lung cancer. Smoking causes emphysema. Smoking while pregnant causes birth defects.* Fairly straightforward stuff. Hard to argue with. And those are just the soft-pedaled American warnings. European cigarette makers place their warnings in coal-black, Magic Marker–thick frames, making them even harder to miss. In Portugal, dwarfing the dromedary on Camel packs, are words even a kid could understand: *Fumar Mata.* Smoking kills. But nothing comes even close to the cigarette warnings from Canada, Thailand, Australia, Brazil—and soon the U.K. They're gorily, forensically true-to-life, showing full-color images of lung tumors, gangrenous feet and toes, and the open sores and disintegrating teeth that accompany mouth and throat cancers.

You'd think these graphic images would stop most smokers in their tracks. So why, in 2006, despite worldwide tobacco advertising bans, outspoken and frequent health warnings from the medical community, and massive government investment in antismoking campaigns, did global consumers continue to smoke a whopping 5,763 billion cigarettes, a figure which doesn't include duty-free cigarettes, or the huge international black market trade? (I was once in an Australian convenience store where I overheard the clerk asking a smoker, "Do you want the pack with the picture of the lungs, the heart, or the feet?" How often did this happen, I asked the clerk? Fifty percent of the time that customers asked for cigarettes, he told me.) Despite what is now known about smoking, it's estimated that about one-third of adult males across the globe continue to light up. Approximately 15 billion cigarettes are sold every day—that's 10 million cigarettes sold a minute. In China, where untold millions of smokers believe that cigarettes can cure Parkinson's disease, relieve symptoms of schizophrenia, boost the efficacy of brain cells, and improve their performance at work, over 300 million people,[1] including 60 percent of all male doctors, smoke. With annual sales of 1.8 trillion cigarettes, the Chinese monopoly is responsible for roughly one-third of all cigarettes being smoked on earth today[2]—a large percentage of the 1.4 billion people using tobacco, which, according to World Bank projections, is expected to increase to roughly 1.6 billion by 2025 (though China consumes more cigarettes than the United States, Russia, Japan, and Indonesia combined).

In the Western world, nicotine addiction still ranks as an enormous concern. Smoking is the biggest killer in Spain today, with fifty thousand smoking-related deaths annually. In the U.K., roughly one-third of all adults under the age of sixty-five light up, while approximately 42 percent of people under sixty-five are exposed to tobacco smoke at home.[3] Twelve times more British people have died from smoking than died in World War II. According to the American Lung Association, smoking-related diseases affect roughly 438,000 American lives a year, "including those affected indirectly, such as babies born prematurely due to prenatal maternal smoking and victims of 'secondhand' exposure to tobacco's carcinogens." The health-care costs in the United States

alone? Over $167 billion a year.⁴ And yet cigarette companies
keep coming up with innovative ways to kill us. For example,
Philip Morris's latest weapon against workplace smoking bans
is Marlboro Intense, a smaller, high-tar cigarette—seven puffs
worth—that can be consumed in stolen moments in between
meetings, phone calls, and PowerPoint presentations.⁵

It makes no sense. Are smokers selectively blind to warning labels? Do they think, to a man or a woman, *Yes, but I'm the
exception here?* Are they showing the world some giant act of
bravado? Do they secretly believe they are immortal? Or do
they know the health dangers and just not care?

That's what I was hoping to use fMRI technology to find
out. The thirty-two smokers in today's study? They were
among the 2,081 volunteers from America, England, Germany, Japan, and the Republic of China that I'd enlisted for
the largest, most revolutionary neuromarketing experiment in
history.

It was twenty-five times larger than any neuromarketing
study ever before attempted. Using the most cutting-edge scientific tools available, it revealed the hidden truths behind
how branding and marketing messages work on the human
brain, how our truest selves react to stimuli at a level far
deeper than conscious thought, and how our unconscious
minds control our behavior (usually the opposite of how we
think we behave). In other words, I'd set off on a quest to in-
vestigate some of the biggest puzzles and issues facing consumers, businesses, advertisers, and governments today.

For example, does product placement really work? (The
answer, I found out, is a qualified no.) How powerful are
brand logos? (Fragrance and sound are more potent than any
logo alone.) Does subliminal advertising still take place? (Yes,

and it probably influenced what you picked up at the convenience store the other day.) Is our buying behavior affected by the world's major religions? (You bet, and increasingly so.) What effect do disclaimers and health warnings have on us? (Read on.) Does sex in advertising work (not really) and how could it possibly get more explicit than it is now? (You just watch.)

Beginning in 2004, from start to finish, our study took up nearly three years of my life, cost approximately $7 million (provided by eight multinational companies), comprised multiple experiments, and involved thousands of subjects from across the globe, as well as two hundred researchers, ten professors and doctors, and an ethics committee. And it employed two of the most sophisticated brain-scanning instruments in the world: the fMRI and an advanced version of the electroencephalograph known as the SST, short for steady-state typography, which tracks rapid brain waves in real time. The research team was overseen by Dr. Gemma Calvert, who holds the Chair in Applied Neuroimaging at the University of Warwick, England, and is the founder of Neurosense in Oxford, and Professor Richard Silberstein, the CEO of Neuro-Insight in Australia. And the results? Well, all I'll say for now is that they'll transform the way you think about how and why you buy.

MARLENE, ONE OF the smokers in the study, took her place lying flat on her back inside the fMRI. The machine made a little ticking sound as the platform rose and locked into place. Marlene looked a little hesitant—who wouldn't?—but managed a gung-ho smile as a technician placed the protective head coil over most of her face in preparation for the first brain scan of the day.

From Marlene's pretesting questionnaire and interview, I knew she was a recently divorced mother of two from Middlesex, and that she'd started smoking at boarding school fifteen years earlier. She thought of herself less as a nicotine addict than a "party smoker," that is, she smoked just a couple of "small" cigarettes during the day, as well as eight to ten more at night.

"Are you affected by the warnings on cigarette packs?" the questionnaire had asked.

"Yes," Marlene had written, twirling her pen around in her fingers as though she was about to ignite the thing.

"Are you smoking less as a consequence of these?"

Another yes. More pen-spinning. I've never been a smoker, but I felt for her.

Her interview answers were clear enough, but now it was time to interview her brain. For those who've never had an MRI, it's not what I'd call the most relaxing or enjoyable experience in the world. The machine is clankingly noisy, lying perfectly still is tedious, and if you're at all prone to panic or claustrophobia, it can feel as if you're being buried alive in a phone booth. Once inside, it's best you remain in a state of yogic calm. Breathe. In, out, in again. You're free to blink and swallow, but you better ignore that itch on your left calf if it kills you. A tic, a jiggle, a fidget, a grimace, body twitching— the slightest movement at all and the results can be compromised. Wedding bands, bracelets, necklaces, nose rings, or tongue studs have to be taken off beforehand, as well. Thanks to the machine's rapacious magnet, any scrap of metal would rip off so fast you wouldn't know what just belted you in the eye.

Marlene was in the scanner for a little over an hour. A small reflective apparatus resembling a car's rearview mirror projected a series of cigarette warning labels from various angles, one after another, on a nearby screen. Asked to rate her desire to smoke during this slideshow, Marlene signaled her responses by pressing down on what's known as a button box—a small black console resembling a hand-sized accordion—as each image flashed by.

We continued to perform brain scans on new subjects over the next month and a half.

Five weeks later, the team leader, Dr. Calvert, presented me with the results. I was, to put it mildly, startled. Even Dr. Calvert was taken aback by the findings: warning labels on the sides, fronts, and backs of cigarette packs had no effect on suppressing the smokers' cravings at all. Zero. In other words, all those gruesome photographs, government regulations, billions of dollars some 123 countries had invested in nonsmoking campaigns, all amounted, at the end of a day, to, well, a big waste of money.

"Are you *sure*?" I kept saying.

"Pretty damn certain," she replied, adding that the statistical validity was as solid as could be.

But this wasn't half as amazing as what Dr. Calvert discovered once she analyzed the results further. Cigarette warnings—whether they informed smokers they were at risk of contracting emphysema, heart disease, or a host of other chronic conditions—had in fact *stimulated* an area of the smokers' brains called the nucleus accumbens, otherwise known as "the craving spot." This region is a chain-link of specialized neurons that lights up when the body desires something—whether it's alcohol, drugs, tobacco, sex, or gambling. When stimulated, the nucleus accumbens requires higher and higher doses to get its fix.

In short, the fMRI results showed that cigarette warning labels not only failed to deter smoking, but by activating the nucleus accumbens, it appeared they actually *encouraged* smokers to light up. We couldn't help but conclude that those same cigarette warning labels intended to curb smoking, reduce cancer, and save lives had instead become a killer marketing tool for the tobacco industry.

Most of the smokers checked off yes when they were asked if warning labels worked—maybe because they thought it was the right answer, or what the researchers wanted to hear, or maybe because they felt guilty about what they knew smoking was doing to their health. But as Dr. Calvert concluded later, it wasn't that our volunteers felt ashamed about what smoking was doing to their bodies; they felt guilty that the labels stimulated their brains' craving areas. It was just that their conscious minds couldn't tell the difference. Marlene hadn't been lying when she filled out her questionnaire. But her brain—the ultimate no-bullshit zone—had adamantly contradicted her. Just as our brains do to each one of us every single day.

The results of the additional brain scan studies I carried out were just as provocative, fascinating, and controversial as the cigarette research project. One by one, they brought me closer to a goal I'd set out to accomplish: to overturn some of the most long-held assumptions, myths, and beliefs about what kinds of advertising, branding, and packaging actually work to arouse our interest and encourage us to buy. If I could

help uncover the subconscious forces that stimulate our interest and ultimately cause us to open our wallets, the brain-scan
study would be the most important three years of my life.

BY WAY OF profession, I'm a global branding expert. That is,
it's been a lifelong mission (and passion) to figure out how
consumers think, why they buy or don't buy the products they
do—and what marketers and advertisers can do to pump new
life into products that are sick, stuck, stumbling, or just lousy
to begin with.

If you look around, chances are pretty good you'll find my
branding fingerprints are all over your house or apartment,
from those products under the kitchen sink, to the chocolate
you stash in your desk drawer, to the phone beside your bed,
to the shaving cream in your bathroom, to the car sitting in the
driveway. Maybe I helped brand your TV's remote control.
The coffee you gulped down this morning. The bacon cheeseburger and French fries you ordered in last week. Your computer software. Your espresso machine. Your toothpaste. Your
dandruff shampoo. Your lip balm. Your underwear. Over the
years I've been doing this work, I've helped brand antiperspi-
rant, feminine hygiene products, iPod speakers, beer, motorcycles, perfume, Saudi Arabian eggs—the list goes on and on.
As a branding expert and brand futurist (meaning that the sum
of my globe-hopping experience gives me a helicopter view
of probable future consumer and advertising trends), businesses consider my colleagues and me something of a brand
ambulance service, a crisis-intervention management team.

Let's say that your line of pricey bottled water from the

Silica-Filled-Crystal-Clear-Mountain-Streams-and-Artesian-Wells-of-Wherever is tanking. The company wants consumers to believe it's bottled by elves standing ankle-deep in fjords rather than inside a sprawling plant off the New Jersey Turnpike, but regardless, its market shares are tumbling, and no one in the company knows what to do. I'll begin digging. What's the secret of their product? What makes it stand out? Are there any stories or rituals or mysteries consumers associate with it? If not, can we root around and find some? Can the product somehow break through the two-dimensional barrier of advertising by appealing to senses the company hasn't yet thought of? Smell, touch, sound? A gasp the cap makes when you unscrew it? A flirty pink straw? Is the advertising campaign edgy and funny and risk-taking, or is it as boring and forgettable as every other company's?

Because I travel so much, I'm able to see how brands perform all over the world. I'm on an airplane about three hundred days out of the year, giving presentations, analyses, and speeches. If it's Tuesday, I could be in Mumbai. The next day São Paolo. Or Dublin, Tokyo, Edinburgh, San Francisco, Athens, Lima, Sri Lanka, or Shanghai. But my hectic travel schedule is an advantage I can bring to a team that's usually too busy to go outside their own building for lunch, much less visit a store in Rio de Janeiro or Amsterdam or Buenos Aires to observe their product in action.

I've been told more times than I can count that my appearance is as nonconventional as what I do for a living. At thirty-eight, I stand about five feet eight inches, and am blessed, or cursed, with an extremely young, boyish-looking face. The excuse I've come up with over the years is that I grew up in Denmark, where it was so cold all the time the weather froze my looks in place. My features, my raked-back blond hair, and my habit of wearing all black give a lot of people the impression that I'm some kind of quirky child evangelist, or maybe some precocious, slightly wired high-school student who got lost on the way to the science lab and ended up in a corporate boardroom by mistake. I've gotten used to this over the years. I suppose you could say that it's evolved into my brand.

So how did I find myself staring through a window into an antiseptic medical lab in a rain-soaked English university as one volunteer after another submitted to an fMRI brain scan?

By 2003, it had become pretty clear to me that traditional research methods, like market research and focus groups, were no longer up to the task of finding out what consumers *really* think. And that's because our irrational minds, flooded with cultural biases rooted in our tradition, upbringing, and a whole lot of other subconscious factors, assert a powerful but hidden influence over the choices we make. Like Marlene and all those other smokers who said that cigarette warnings discouraged them from smoking, we may *think* we know why we do the things we do—but a much closer look into the brain tells us otherwise.

Think about it. As human beings, we enjoy thinking of ourselves as a rational species. We feed and clothe ourselves. We go to work. We remember to turn down the thermostat at night. We download music. We go to the gym. We handle crises—missed deadlines, a child falling off a bike, a friend getting sick, a parent dying, etc.—in a grown-up, evenhanded way. At the least, that's our goal. If a partner or colleague accuses us of acting irrationally, we get a little offended. They might as well have just accused us of temporary insanity.

But like it or not, all of us consistently engage in behavior for which we have no logical or clear-cut explanation. This is truer than ever before in our stressed-out, technologically overwired world, where news of terrorist threats, political saber-rattling, fires, earthquakes, floods, violence, and assorted other disasters pelts us from the moment we turn on the morning news to the time we go to bed. The more stress we're under, the more frightened and insecure and uncertain we feel—and the more irrationally we tend to behave.

For example, consider how much superstition governs our lives. We knock on wood for luck. (I've been in boardrooms where, if there's no wood around, executives will glance around helplessly for a substitute. Does a briefcase count? A pencil? What about the floor?) We won't walk under ladders. We cross our fingers for luck. We'd prefer not to fly on Friday the thirteenth, or drive down the street where we spotted that black cat in the bushes last week. If we break a mirror, we think, *That's it, seven years of bad luck.* Of course, if you ask us, most of us will say no, don't be ridiculous, I give absolutely no credence to any of those inane superstitions. Yet most of us continue to act on them, every day of our lives.

Under stress (or even when life is going along pretty well), people tend to say one thing while their behavior suggests something entirely different. Needless to say, this spells disaster for the field of market research, which relies on consumers being accurate and honest. But 85 percent of the time our brains are on autopilot. It's not that we mean to lie—it's just that our unconscious minds are a lot better at interpreting our behavior (including why we buy) than our conscious minds are.

The concept of brand-building has been around for close

to a century. But advertisers still don't know much more than department store pioneer John Wanamaker did a century ago when he famously declared, "Half my advertising budget is wasted. Trouble is, I don't know which half." Companies often don't know what to do to engage us authentically—as opposed to simply attracting our attention. I'm not saying companies aren't smart, because they are. Some, like the tobacco companies, are *scarily* smart. But most still can't answer a basic question: What drives us, as consumers, to make the choices we do? What causes us to choose one brand or product over another? What are shoppers really thinking? And since no one can come up with a decent answer to these questions, companies plow ahead using the same strategies and techniques as they always have. Marketers, for example, are still doing the same old stuff: quantitative research, which involves surveying lots and lots of volunteers about an idea, a concept, a product, or even a kind of packaging—followed by qualitative research, which turns a more intense spotlight on smaller focus groups handpicked from the same population. In 2005, corporations spent more than $7.3 billion on market research in the United States alone. In 2007, that figure rose to $12 billion. And that doesn't even include the additional expenses involved in marketing an actual product—the packaging and displays, TV commercials, online banner ads, celebrity endorsements, and billboards—which carry a $117 billion annual price tag in America alone.

But if those strategies still work, then why do eight out of ten new product launches fail within the first three months? (In Japan, product launches fail a miserable 9.7 times out of every ten.) What we know now, and what you'll read about in the pages that follow, is that what people say on surveys and in focus groups does *not* reliably affect how they behave—far from it. Let's take an example. Today's modern mother is more and more fearful about "germs," "safety," and "health." No woman in her right mind wants to accidentally ingest *E. coli,* or pick up strep throat, nor does she want little Ethan or Sophie to get infected either. So a company's research department develops a small vial of something antibacterial—we'll call it "Pure-Al"—that women can tuck in their pockets, and whip out to slather on their hands after a day spent in a suffocating office, a friend's filthy apartment or an overcrowded subway car.

But can Pure-Al really inhibit our fears about "germs" and "safety"? How can its marketers know what these terms mean to most of us? Sure, there's a basic human desire to feel safe and secure, as well as a natural aversion to germ-ridden banisters, bacteria-laden jungle gyms, and dusty offices. But as our smokers' questionnaires showed, we don't always express or act on these feelings consciously; there's an entire peninsula of thought and feeling that remains out of reach. The same goes for every single other emotion we experience, whether it's love, empathy, jealousy, anger, revulsion, and so on.

Tiny, barely perceptible factors can slant focus group responses. Maybe one woman felt that as a mother of four kids and three dogs and seventeen geckos, she *should* care more about germs, but didn't want to admit to the other women in the room that her house was already messy beyond the pale. Or maybe the head of the research team reminded another woman of an ex-boyfriend who left her for her best friend and this (okay, just maybe) tainted her impression of the product.

Maybe they just all hated his nose.

Point is, try putting *these* micro-emotions into words or writing them down in a roomful of strangers. It can't be done. That's why the true reactions and emotions we as consumers experience are more likely to be found in the brain, in the nanosecond lapse before thinking is translated into words. So, if marketers want the naked truth—the truth, unplugged and uncensored, about what causes us to buy—they have to interview our brains.

All of this is why, in 2003, I became convinced that something was fundamentally wrong with the ways companies reached out to customers, to us. Quite simply, companies didn't seem to understand consumers. Companies couldn't find and develop brands that matched our needs. Nor were they sure how to communicate in a way so that their products gripped our minds and hearts. Whether they were marketing cosmetics, pharmaceuticals, fast-food, cars, or pickles, no advertisers dared to stand out, or to try out anything remotely new or revolutionary. In terms of understanding the mind of the average consumer they were like Christopher Columbus in 1492, gripping a torn, hand-drawn map as the wind picked up and his boat lurched and listed toward what might or might not be flat land.

By uncovering the brain's deepest secrets, I wasn't interested in helping companies manipulate consumers—far from it. I buy a lot of stuff, too, after all, and at the end of the day, I'm as susceptible to products and brands as anyone. I also want to sleep well at night, knowing I've done the right thing (over the years I've turned down projects that, in my opinion, crossed that line). By attempting to shine a spotlight on the buying behavior of over two thousand study subjects, I felt I could help uncover our minds' truest motivations—and just maybe push human brain science forward at the same time.

It was time to throw everything up in the air, see where it landed, then start all over again. Which is where our brain-scanning study came in.

FOR ME, IT all began with a *Forbes* magazine cover story, "In Search of the Buy Button," which I picked up during a typical daylong airplane flight. The article chronicled the goings-on in a small lab in Greenwich, England, where a market researcher had joined forces with a cognitive neuroscientist to peer inside the brains of eight young women as they watched a TV show interspersed with half-a-dozen or so commercials for products ranging from Kit Kat chocolates, to Smirnoff vodka, to Volkswagen's Passat.

Using a technique known as SST, which measures electrical activity inside the brain (and resembles, I later found out, a floppy black Roaring Twenties–era bathing cap), the scientist and researcher had focused on a sequence of wiry lines crawling across a computer, like two garter snakes engaged in a mating dance. Only these weren't snakes, but brain waves, which SST was measuring millisecond-by-millisecond, in real time, as the volunteers viewed the commercials. An abrupt spike in one woman's left prefrontal cortex might indicate to researchers that she found Kit Kats appealing or appetizing. A sharp drop later on, and the neurologist might infer the last thing in the world she wanted was a Smirnoff-on-the-rocks.[6]

Brain waves as calibrated by SST are straight shooters.

They don't waver, hold back, equivocate, cave in to peer pressure, conceal their vanity, or say what they think the person across the table wants to hear. No: like fMRI, SST was the final word on the human mind. You couldn't get any more cutting-edge than this. In other words, neuroimaging could uncover truths that a half-century of market research, focus groups, and opinion polling couldn't come close to accomplishing.

I was so excited by what I was reading I nearly rang the call button just so I could tell the steward.

As I mentioned earlier, eight out of every ten products launched in the United States are destined to fail. In 2005, more than 156,000 new products debuted in stores globally, the equivalent of one new product release every three minutes.[7] Globally, according to the IXP Marketing Group, roughly 21,000 new brands are introduced worldwide per year, yet history tells us that all but a few of them have vanished from the shelf a year later.[8] In consumer products alone, 52 percent of all new brands, and 75 percent of individual products, fail.[9] Pretty terrible numbers. Neuroimaging, I realized, could zero in on those with the highest chance of succeeding by pinpointing consumers' reward centers and revealing which marketing or advertising efforts were most stimulating, appealing, or memorable, and which ones were dull, off-putting, anxiety-provoking, or worst of all, forgettable.

Market research wasn't going away, but it was about to take a seat at the neuroscience table and in the process, take on a brainy new look.

*   *   *

IN 1975, WATERGATE was still scandalizing America. Margaret Thatcher was elected the leader of the conservative party in Great Britain. Color TV debuted in Australia. Bruce Springsteen came out with *Born to Run.* And executives at the Pepsi-Cola Company decided to roll out a heavily publicized experiment known as the Pepsi Challenge. It was very simple. Hundreds of Pepsi reps set up tables in malls and supermarkets all over the world, handing out two unmarked cups to every man, woman, and child who'd stopped to see what all the commotion was about. One cup contained Pepsi, the other Coke. The subjects were asked which one they preferred. If the results worked out as they hoped, Pepsi might finally make a dent in Coke's longtime domination of the estimated $68 billion U.S. soft drink industry.

When the company's marketing department finally toted up the results, Pepsi executives were pleased, if slightly perplexed. More than half of the volunteers claimed to prefer the taste of Pepsi over Coke. Hallelujah, right? So by all accounts, Pepsi should be trouncing Coke all across the world. But it wasn't. It made no sense.

In his 2005 best-seller, *Blink,* Malcolm Gladwell offers a partial interpretation. The Pepsi Challenge was a "Sip Test," or what's known in the soda industry as a "Central Location Test," or CLT. He cites a former Pepsi new-product development executive, Carol Dollard, who explains the difference between taking a sip of a soft drink out of a cup and downing the entire can. In a sip test, people tend to like the sweeter product—in this case Pepsi—but when they drink an entire can of the stuff, there always lurks the possibility of blood sugar–overkill. That, according to Gladwell, is why Pepsi prevailed in the taste test, but Coke continued to lead the market.[10]

But in 2003, Dr. Read Montague, the director of the Human Neuroimaging Lab at Baylor College of Medicine in Houston, decided to probe the test results more deeply. Twenty-eight years after the original Pepsi Challenge, he revised the study, this time using fMRI to measure the brains of his sixty-seven study subjects. First, he asked the volunteers whether they preferred Coke, Pepsi, or had no preference whatsoever. The results matched the findings of the original experiment almost exactly; more than half of the test subjects reported a marked preference for Pepsi. Their brains did, too. While taking a sip of Pepsi, this entirely new set of volunteers registered a flurry of activity in the ventral putamen, a region of the brain that's stimulated when we find tastes appealing.

Interesting, but not all that dramatic—until a fascinating finding showed up in the second stage of the experiment.

This time around, Dr. Montague decided to let the test subjects know whether they were sampling Pepsi or Coke *before* they tasted it. The result: 75 percent of the respondents claimed to prefer Coke. What's more, Montague also observed a change in the location of their brain activity. In addition to the ventral putamen, blood flows were now registering in the medial prefrontal cortex, a portion of the brain responsible, among other duties, for higher thinking and discernment. All this indicated to Dr. Montague that two areas in the brain were engaged in a mute tug-of-war between rational and emotional thinking. And during that mini-second of grappling and indecision, the emotions rose up like mutinous soldiers to override respondents' rational preference for Pepsi. And that's the moment Coke won.[11]

All the positive associations the subjects had with Coca-Cola—its history, logo, color, design, and fragrance; their own childhood memories of Coke, Coke's TV and print ads over the years, the sheer, inarguable, inexorable, ineluctable, emotional *Coke*-ness of the brand—beat back their rational, natural preference for the taste of Pepsi. Why? Because emotions are the way in which our brains encode things of value, and a brand that engages us emotionally—think Apple, Harley-Davidson, and L'Oréal, just for starters—will win every single time.

That Dr. Montague's study had proven a conclusive scientific link between branding and the brain took the scientific community by surprise . . . and you can bet advertisers began paying attention, too. A newborn but intriguing window into our thought patterns and decision-making processes was a few sips closer to becoming reality.

A similar, but no less powerful neuromarketing experiment soon followed on the heels of the Coke–Pepsi study. Far north from Texas, four Princeton University psychologists were busy conducting another experiment, this one aimed at scanning subjects' brains as they were presented with a choice: short-term immediate gratification versus delayed rewards.

The psychologists asked a group of random students to choose between a pair of Amazon.com gift vouchers. If they picked the first, a $15 gift voucher, they would get it at once. If they were willing to wait two weeks for the $20 gift certificate, well, obviously they'd be getting more bang for their buck. The brain scans revealed that both gift options triggered activity in the lateral prefrontal cortex, the area of the brain that generates emotion. But the possibility of getting that $15 gift certificate *now!* caused an unusual flurry of stimulation in the limbic areas of most students' brains—a whole grouping of brain structures that's primarily responsible for our emotional life, as well as for the formation of memory. The more the students were emotionally excited about something, the psychologists found, the greater the chances of their opting for the immediate, if less immediately gratifying, alternative. Of course, their rational minds knew the $20 was logically a better deal, but—guess what—their emotions won out.[12]

Economists, too, want to understand the underlying decisions involved in what makes us behave as we do. Economic theory may be fairly sophisticated, but it's come up against blocks similar to the ones advertising is confronting. "Finance and economic research has hit the wall," explains Andrew Lo, who runs AlphaSimplex Group, a Cambridge, Massachusetts, hedge fund firm. "We need to get inside the brain to understand why people make decisions."[13]

That's because, just like market research, economic modeling is based on the premise that people behave in a predictably rational way. But again, what's beginning to show up in the fledgling world of brain scanning is the enormous influences our emotions have on every decision we make. Thus the interest in neuro-economics, the study of the way the brain makes financial decisions. Thanks to fMRI, it is giving unprecedented insight into how emotions—such as generosity, greed, fear, and well-being—impact economic decision-making.

As George Loewenstein, a behavioral economist from Carnegie Mellon University, confirmed: "Most of the brain is dominated by automatic processes, rather than deliberate thinking. A lot of what happens in the brain is emotional, not cognitive."[14]

*   *   *

IT COMES AS no surprise that once neuroimaging had snagged the attention of the advertising world, it would find its way into other disciplines, too. In fact, politics, law enforcement, economics, and even Hollywood were already in on the action.

Politicians' interest in the fMRI—well, you could almost see it coming. Committees spend up to a billion dollars handcrafting an electable presidential candidate—and elections are increasingly won and lost by the tiniest fraction of a percentage point. Imagine having at your disposal a tool that could possibly pinpoint what goes on in the brains of registered voters. If you were involved in a campaign, you'd want to use it, right? Or so Tom Freedman, a strategist and senior advisor to the Clinton administration, must have thought when he founded a company known as FKF Applied Research. FKF is devoted to studying decision-making processes, and how the brain responds to leadership qualities. In 2003, his company used fMRI scanning to analyze public responses to campaign commercials during the run-up to the Bush-Kerry presidential campaign.

Freedman's test subjects looked at a selection of commercials for incumbent president George W. Bush and Massachusetts senator John Kerry; photographs of each candidate; images of the September 11 World Trade Center terrorist attacks; and former president Lyndon Johnson's infamous 1964 "Daisy" ad in which a young girl is seen frolicking with a daisy as a nuclear explosion detonates.

The results? Not surprisingly, the September 11 attack imagery and the "Daisy" ad triggered a noticeable, across-the-board increase in activity in voters' amygdalas, a small brain region named after the Greek word for "almond," which governs, among other things, fear, anxiety, and dread. Yet

Freedman found that Republicans and Democrats reacted differently to ads replaying the September 11 attacks; the amygdalas of Democrats lit up far more noticeably than the amygdalas of Republicans. Marco Iacobini, the lead researcher and an associate professor at the Neuropsychiatric Institute, interpreted this odd discrepancy to Democrats' fear that 9/11 was a nerve-wracking touch-point that could lead to George W. Bush's reelection in 2004. Tom Freedman threw in the theory that in general, Democrats are a lot more unsettled by the idea of military force, which they associated with 9/11, than are most Republicans.

But what was most interesting to Freedman was that his study also showed that scanning voters' amygdalas could be beneficial in designing campaign ads, as playing on voters' fear has been shown time and time again to be key in securing a politician's win. After all, Johnson's "Daisy" ad had helped to ensure his victory in 1964 by playing to the fear of nuclear war. And, as it turned out, history would repeat itself forty years later when the Republicans clinched victory in the 2004 election by sledgehammering the fear of terrorism into voters' heads. Despite widespread cries that political advertising emphasize "optimism," "hope," "building up, not tearing down," and so on, fear works. It's what our brains remember.

Although using brain-scanning technology to sway political decisions is in its infancy, I predict that the 2008 American presidential showdown will be the last-ever election to be governed by traditional surveys, and that by 2012, neuroscience will begin to dominate *all* election predictions. "These new tools could help us someday be less reliant on clichés and unproven adages. They'll help put a bit more science in political science," Tom Freedman commented.[15]

Hollywood, too, is fascinated by neuroscience. A Stanford University experimental neurobiologist, Steve Quartz, has studied subjects' brains to see how they respond to trailers of movies that are weeks, if not months, away from general release. Are they memorable, catchy, provocative? Will they hook our attention? By exploring precisely what appeals to the brain's reward center, studios can create the most provocative trailers, or even sculpt the end of the movie to reflect what appeals to us, the viewing public.[16] So if you think films are formulaic now, fasten your seatbelts for *Rocky 52*.

As for law enforcement? One California entrepreneur has come up with a neuroimaging spin on the widely used polygraph, or lie-detector, test with a product called the No Lie MRI. Its assumption, as any capable dissembler can tell you, is that it takes effort to lie. In other words, saying, "No, I didn't cheat on you, darling," or "I *swear* I used my blinker!" requires a stimulation of cognition—and thus a rush of oxygenated blood to the brain. Even the U.S. Pentagon has increased their research into an MRI-based lie detection program, partially funded by the Defense Advanced Research Projects Agency, which comes up with ingenious new tools and techniques for military use.[17]

But back to marketing. As we've seen, this fledgling science had already made some inroads. In 2002, for example, Daimler-Chrysler's research center in the German town of Ulm used fMRIs to study the brains of consumers while showing them images of a series of automobiles, including Mini Coopers and Ferraris. And what they found was that as the subjects gazed at a slide of a Mini Cooper, a discrete region in the back area of the brain that responds to faces came alive. The fMRI had just pinpointed the essence of the Mini

Cooper's appeal. Above and beyond the car's "wide bulldog stance," "ultra-rigid body," "1.6L 16-valve alloy engine," and "6 airbags with side protection" (goodies lauded on the car's Web site),[18] the Mini Cooper registered in subjects' brains as an adorable face. It was a gleaming little person, Bambi on four wheels, or Pikachu with an exhaust pipe. You just wanted to pinch its little fat metallic cheeks, then drive it away.

There's no doubt that babies' faces have a strong effect on our brains. In a University of Oxford study involving an imaging technique known as magnetoencephalography, neuroscientist Morten L. Kringelbach asked 12 adults to carry out a computer task while the faces of infants and adults (similar in expression) flashed onto a nearby screen. According to *Scientific American,* "While the volunteers ultimately processed the faces using the brain regions that normally handle such a task, all the participants showed an early, distinct response to the infant faces alone." More specifically, "Within one-seventh of a second, a spike in activity occurred in the medial orbitofrontal cortex, an area above the eye sockets linked to the detection of rewarding stimuli." In other words, according to Kringelbach, the volunteers' brains seemed to identify infants' faces as somehow special.[19]

More intriguing revelations followed. Daimler-Chrysler researchers then displayed images of sixty-six different cars to a dozen men, again scanning their brains using the fMRI. This time, the sports cars stimulated the region of the brain associated with "reward and reinforcement" according to Henrik Walter, a psychiatrist and neuroscientist involved in the study. And what is often the most rewarding thing for guys? Sex. It seemed, just as male peacocks attract female mates with the iridescence of their back feathers, the males in this study subconsciously sought to attract the opposite sex with the low-rising, engine-revving, chrome pizzazz of the sports car. Walter even took it one step further, explaining that just as female birds reject male birds with scrawny plumages—the peacock-equivalent of a comb-over—in favor of the most preening, showstopping birds because the length and sheen of a male peacock's plumage correlate directly to the bird's vigor, virility, and social status, so do women prefer men with a showy, slinky sports car: "If you are strong and successful as an animal, you can afford to invest energy in such a pointless thing," Walter points out.

In essence, neuroscience revealed what I'd always believed: that brands are much more than just recognizable products wrapped in eye-catching designs. Yet at the time, all previous neuroimaging tests had focused on a particular product. The brain scan study I decided to undertake would be the first attempt to examine not just a specific brand—whether a Heineken, a Honda Civic, a Gillette razor, or a Q-tip—but to explore what the concept "brand" really means to our brains. If I could sneak a peek inside consumers' heads to find out why some products worked, while others fell flat on their faces, I knew my study could not only transform the way companies designed, marketed, and advertised their products—but also help each one of us understand what is *really* going on inside our brains when we make decisions about what we buy.

So what the heck was I supposed to do next?

The obvious next stage was to find the best scientists—and the most sophisticated instruments around—to help me carry out this experiment. Ultimately, I decided to combine two methods, SST, the advanced version of the electroencephalograph; and fMRI. I chose these for a number of reasons. Neither instrument is invasive. Neither involves radiation. And both are able to measure the level of emotional attraction (or revulsion) we as consumers experience more precisely than any other tool available.

FMRI, as I mentioned earlier, is able to pinpoint an area as small as one millimeter in the brain. In essence, it takes a miniature home movie of the brain every few seconds—and in as little as ten minutes can amass a spectacular amount of information. Meanwhile, the less expensive SST brings with it the advantage of being able to measure reactions instantaneously (while fMRI has a few seconds delay). This made SST ideal for registering brain activity while people are watching TV commercials and programs, or any other kind of visual stimuli happening in real time. Better yet, it's portable and travel ready—a kind of movable laboratory (which, believe me, came in handy when we secured special, unprecedented permission from the Chinese government to scan the brains of Chinese consumers).

Ultimately, we based our research on 102 fMRI scans and 1,979 SST studies. Why not half-and-half? A typical fMRI brain scan, which involves design, analysis, conducting the experiment, and interpreting the results, can be expensive. SST studies are far less costly. Even so, our fMRI studies were almost twice as extensive as any conducted to date.

Until we began our research, no one had ever mixed and matched fMRI and SST on behalf of a broad-scale neuro-marketing study. If you think of the brain as a house, any and all previous experiments were based on looking through a single window, but our wide-ranging study promised to cast its gaze through as many windows, cracks, floorboards, attic windows, and mouse holes as we could find.

But this study wasn't going to come cheap, and I knew that without corporate backing, it was dead in the water. But when I get an idea in my head that keeps me up at night, I'm persistent. Politely pushy, you might call it. Those twenty-seven messages on your answering machine? They're all from me (sorry). Nevertheless, in spite of all my efforts, business after business turned me down. The people I approached were either intrigued-but-unconvinced, or intrigued-but-spooked. And of course, with a brain-scanning experiment this ambitious, backers weren't without their ethical concerns. "Orwellian"—that's the most frequently heard reaction when people hear the word *neuromarketing*. A recent *New York Times Magazine* cover story touching on the law and brain imaging noted a widespread fear among scholars that brain scanning is a "kind of super mind-reading device" that threatens the privacy and "mental freedom" of citizens.[20]

But to be honest, I didn't share these ethical concerns. As I said in the introduction, neuromarketing isn't about implanting ideas in people's brains, or forcing them to buy what they don't want to buy; it's about uncovering what's already inside our heads—our Buyology. Our willing volunteers were genuinely excited to take part in the birth of a new science. There were no complaints. No adverse reactions, no side effects, no health risks. Everyone knew what they were doing, and they were fully briefed before they signed on. And in the end, a hospital ethics committee oversaw every detail and aspect of our study, ensuring that nothing could go forward until we'd cleared it with them first.

Finally, one company said they were willing to give neuromarketing a shot. Followed by another company. Then another. A few months later, I'd secured all the resources I needed from eight multinational corporations. Finally, I put in some money of my own.

Now, I was faced with the largest operational and logistical headache I've ever come up against: finding a huge number of volunteers—2,081 at final count—from a handful of countries around the world. Why? First, I didn't want anyone claiming that the sample population I came up with was in any way too narrow or limited. Plus, our research had to be global, because the work I do is global, and because in today's world, companies and brands are global as well.

So I settled on a final five countries: America, because it's home to Madison Avenue and Hollywood; Germany, because it's the most advanced country in the world as far as neuromarketing is concerned; England, because it's where Dr. Calvert's company is based; Japan, because there's no rougher, tougher place in the world to launch a new product; and China, because it's by far the world's largest emerging market.

Cut to a few months later, when I found myself in a Los Angeles studio, surrounded by hundreds of volunteers, attired in SST caps, electrodes, wires, and goggles, all glued to a TV screen watching Simon Cowell, Paula Abdul, and Randy Jackson perched in their red chairs like a high-school disciplinary committee. Simon idly sipped a Coke as across the stage, a guy with sideburns and a Hawaiian shirt warbled an off-key rendition of the Monkees' "Daydream Believer."

By exploring viewers' responses to one of the most popular TV shows in America, our first experiment would answer the first question I was posing—does product placement really work, or was it, despite what advertisers and consumers alike have long believed, a colossal waste of money?

2

Product Placement, American
Idol, *and Ford's Multimillion-
Dollar Mistake*

REMEMBER THAT COM-
mercial you saw on *American Idol* two nights ago? The one
where the tractor salesman was scarfing down those fish
sticks, and that kind-of-funny cell phone ad with those two
quacking ducks . . .

Yeah, me neither. As a matter of fact, I don't even remember what I had for dinner two nights ago. Steak? Lasagna? Fet-
tucine Alfredo? A Caesar salad? Maybe I forgot to eat. The
point is, I can't recall—just as I have no recollection of the
third man who landed on the moon, or the fourth person who
summited Mt. Everest.

By the time we reach the age of sixty-six, most of us will
have seen approximately two million television commercials.
Time-wise, that's the equivalent of watching eight hours of
ads seven days a week for six years straight. In 1965 a typical
consumer had a 34 percent recall of those ads. In 1990, that
figure had fallen to 8 percent. A 2007 ACNielsen phone survey of one thousand consumers found that the average per-

son could name a mere 2.21 commercials of those they had ever seen, ever, period.[1] Today, if I ask most people what companies sponsored their favorite TV shows—say, *Lost* or *House* or *The Office*—their faces go blank. They can't remember a single one. I don't blame them. Goldfish, I read once, have a working memory of approximately seven seconds—so every seven seconds, they start their lives all over again. Reminds me of the way I feel when I watch TV commercials.

A couple of reasons for this jump out at me right away. The first and most obvious is today's fast-moving, ever-changing, always-on media assault. The Internet with its pop-ups and banner ads, cable TV, twenty-four-hour news stations, newspapers, magazines, catalogs, e-mail, iPods, podcasts, instant messaging, text-messaging, and computer and video games are all vying for our increasingly finite and worn-out attention spans. As a result, the filtering system in our brains has grown thick and self-protective. We're less and less able to recall what we saw on TV just this morning, forget about a couple of nights ago.

Another no less important factor behind our amnesia is the pervasive lack of originality on the part of advertisers. Their reasoning is simple: If what we've been doing has worked for years, why shouldn't we just keep on doing it? Which is a little like saying, if I'm a baseball player who's been striking out regularly for the past decade, why should I bother changing my swing, or altering my stance, or gripping the bat a little differently? A few years ago, I conducted a small experiment—a little narrower in scope than my brain-scan experiment—on my own. I taped sixty different TV car commercials produced by twenty different automotive companies. Each one had been running on TV for the past two years. Each one had a scene in which the new, shiny, and seemingly driverless car guns its way around a hairpin turn in the desert, sending up a dramatic little cloud of dust—*poof.* The thing is, though the make of car might have differed, that scene was exactly the same in every single commercial. Same swerve. Same turn. Same desert. Same dust cloud. Just for fun, I created a montage of these breathtakingly unmemorable moments on a two-minute reel, to see if I could tell which car was a Toyota, a Nissan, a Honda, an Audi, or a Subaru. And indeed, when I watched the tape, turns out I was stumped. I couldn't tell one car from the other.

It was, and is, a depressingly true-to-life example of what's going on today in TV commercials. There's no originality out there—it's too risky. Uncreative companies are simply imitating other uncreative companies. In the end, everyone's a loser because we as TV viewers can't tell one brand from the next. We watch commercial after commercial, but the only thing we're left with, if they've registered in our memories at all, is the image of a shiny, anonymous car and a handful of dust.

ON JUNE 11, 2002, a popular British TV show known as *Pop Idol* made the transatlantic crossing to the United States, and in its retitled debut as *American Idol* became one of the most popular and successful shows in American television history virtually overnight. (The story goes that it never would have been aired in the United States if Rupert Murdoch's daughter, a huge fan of the show, hadn't persuaded her father to take a chance on it. She knew what she was doing.)

By now, most of us know how the show works. In its first

few weeks, the producers and cast of *American Idol* city-hop around the United States, auditioning aspiring singers whose talent levels range from expert-but-needs-work, to promising, to at times wincingly bad. Over the course of the season, the show's three judges eliminate all but twenty-four contestants, until finally the home-viewing audience gets the chance to vote each week, with the contestant with the fewest votes getting kicked off. At the end of the season, the last one standing becomes the next American Idol.

But what do aspiring singers, snarky judges, and dreams of fame, glory, and stardom have to do with the next part of our study? Everything. Until now, I'd only suspected that traditional advertising and marketing strategies like commercials and product placement didn't work—but now it was time to put them to the ultimate test.

American Idol has three main sponsors, Cingular Wireless (which has since been bought by AT&T, but I'll refer to it in this chapter as Cingular because that was its name at the time the ads ran), the Ford Motor Company, and Coca-Cola, each of whom fork over an estimated $26 million annually to have their brands featured on one of the highest-rated shows in television history.

And this is only a small part of an enormous and expensive worldwide industry. According to a study conducted by PQ Media, in 2006, companies paid a total of $3.36 billion globally to have their products featured in various TV shows, music videos, and movies. In 2007, this increased to $4.38 billion and is predicted to reach a whopping $7.6 billion by 2010.[2] That's a whole lot of money, given that this would be the first time that the effectiveness of product placement has ever been scientifically tested or validated. As I mentioned, I can't remember what I ate for dinner the other night, much less the Honda commercial I saw on TV yesterday. So who's to say I'll remember what soft drink Simon Cowell was sipping as he leaned forward, eyes gleaming, to lambaste yet another poor soul's rendition of Alicia Keys's "Fallin' "?

As viewers, we used to be able to tell the difference between products that somehow play a role or part in a TV show or movie (known in advertising circles as Product Integration) and the standard thirty-second advertising spots that run during the commercial breaks (known as, well, commercials). But increasingly, these two kinds of ads are becoming harder and harder to separate.

On *American Idol,* Coke and Cingular Wireless not only run thirty-second ads during commercial breaks, they also feature their products prominently *during* the show itself. (When asked by a fellow judge if he liked a contestant's song during the February 21, 2008, broadcast, Simon commented, "How much I love Coca-Cola!"—and then took a sip.) The three judges all keep cups of America's most iconic soft drink in front of them, and both the judges and the contestants sit on chairs or couches with rounded contours specifically designed to look like a bottle of Coca-Cola. Before and after their auditions, contestants enter (or exit in a foul-mouthed rage) a room whose walls are painted a chirpy, unmistakable Coca-Cola red. Whether through semi-subtle imagery or traditional advertising spots, Coca-Cola is present approximately 60 percent of the time on *American Idol.*

Cingular, too, pops up repeatedly throughout the show, though to a lesser extent. As the host, Ryan Seacrest, repeatedly reminds us, viewers can dial in, or vote for their favorite contestant via text-message, from a Cingular Wireless cell phone—the only carrier that permits *Idol* voting via text-messaging (text messages from other cell phone providers are evidently discarded, meaning you either have to call in for a fee or forever hold your peace). What's more, the Cingular logo—which looks like an orange cat splattered on a road—shows up alongside every set of phone and text-messaging numbers shown onscreen.[3] And to further cement the relationship between the show and the brand, in 2006 Cingular announced it would begin offering ring tones of live performances from the previous night's show to download to their mobile phones. The cost: $2.95.[4]

Of the show's three main sponsors, Ford is the only advertiser that doesn't share an actual stage with the contestants. Ford's $26 million goes only toward traditional thirty-second ad spots (though in 2006 Ford announced that it had hired American Idol Taylor Hicks—the gray-haired guy—to record a relentlessly up-tempo, feel-good song for both TV and radio entitled "Possibilities" to promote the company's new "Drive On Us" end-of-year sales event). During the show's sixth season, Ford also produced original music videos featuring the company's cars which ran during the commercial breaks in each of the final eleven shows and partnered with the *American Idol* Web site for a weekly sweepstakes promotion.[5]

What's with this relentless advertising assault? In part, it can be attributed to advertisers' calculated end-run against popular new technologies like TiVo, which allows viewers to skip over the TV commercials and watch their favorite shows without interruption. "The shift from programmer- to consumer-controlling program choices is the biggest change in the media business in the past 25 or 30 years," Jeff Gaspin, the president of NBC Universal Television Group, has been quoted as saying.[6] In essence, sponsors are letting us know that it's futile to hide, duck, dodge, fast-forward, or take an extended bathroom break: they'll get to us *somehow*.

But do they? Do all these meticulously planned, shrewdly placed products really penetrate our long-term memory and leave any lasting impression on us at all? Or are they what I like to call "wallpaper" ads—instantly forgettable, the advertising equivalent of elevator Muzak? That's what the next part of our brain study would find out.

THE SETUP WAS simple. Our four hundred carefully chosen subjects were each fitted with a black, turban-like cap wired with a dozen electrodes that resembled tea candles. Researchers then adjusted and looped the wires over their heads, and finally topped off the ensemble with a pair of viewing goggles. In their SST garb, our study subjects looked like random members of an affable Roswell, New Mexico, cult, or a bunch of participants at a psychic fair.

But there was nothing otherworldly or left-to-chance about this study, the first ever to assess the power (or pointlessness) of this billion-dollar product placement industry. The electrodes had been positioned over specific portions of our subjects' brains so that from several feet away, behind a pane of glass, the research team could view—and mathematically measure—exactly what their brain waves were doing in real time. Among other things, SST could measure the degree of subjects' emotional engagement (how interested they were in what they were watching), memory (what parts of what they were watching were penetrating long-term memory), and approach and withdraw (what attracted or repelled them about the visual image). Or in the head researcher Professor Silberstein's words, SST would reveal "how different parts of the brain talk to one another."

The subjects took their seats in a darkened room, and the curtains went up.

PRODUCT PLACEMENT IN movies is as old as the medium itself. Even the pioneering Lumière brothers, two of the world's first filmmakers, included several appearances of Lever's sunlight soap in their early short films. Turns out, they had an associate on staff who moonlighted as a publicist for Lever Brothers (now Unilever). But product placement truly began to blossom in the 1930s. In 1932, White Owl Cigars provided $250,000 worth of advertising for the 1932 film *Scarface,* on the condition that star Paul Muni would smoke them in the movie. By the mid-1940s, it was rare to see a kitchen in a Warner Brothers film that didn't have a spanking-new General Electric refrigerator, or a love story that didn't end in a man presenting a woman with diamonds in a romantic display of undying devotion—the diamonds, of course, being sponsored by the DeBeers Company.[7]

Still, product placement as most of us know it today can be traced back to a little alien. For those who've never seen Steven Spielberg's *E.T.: The Extra-Terrestrial,* the story revolves around a solitary, fatherless boy named Elliott who discovers an extraordinary-looking creature living in the woods behind his house. To lure it out of hiding, the boy tactically places individual pieces of candy—instantly recognizable as Hershey's

Reese's Pieces—along the path from the forest leading into his house.

But Spielberg didn't choose this particular candy at random. The director first approached the Mars Company, the makers of M&Ms, to ask if they'd be willing to pay to have their product featured in the film. After they turned him down, Hershey agreed to step in, offering their Reese's Pieces as a substitute. A very smart corporate decision, as it turns out—a week after the movie's debut, sales of Reese's Pieces tripled, and within a couple of months of its release, more than eight hundred cinemas across the country began stocking Reese's Pieces in their concession stands for the first time.

Enter Tom Cruise. In the late 1970s and early '80s, the U.S.-based sunglasses manufacturer Ray-Ban was fighting to stay alive as their sales figures remained dismally flat. That is, until the company struck a deal with Paul Brickman, the director of 1983's *Risky Business,* and Tom Cruise gave the retro-looking shades a whole lot of renewed cachet. When the movie became a hit, Ray-Ban sales rose by over 50 percent.

But Cruise and his shades were just getting started. Three years later, in Tony Scott's *Top Gun,* when the actor alit from his fighter jet clad in Air Force leathers and Aviator Ray-Bans, the sunglasses maker saw an additional boost of 40 percent to its bottom line. (It wasn't just dark glasses that benefited from the success of *Top Gun.* Sales of leather aviator jackets surged as well, as did Air Force and Navy recruitment, the latter increasing by 500 percent.)

Ray-Ban's success with product placement was reenacted again two decades later. In the six months after Will Smith wore what were now *extremely* retro shades in the 2002 film *Men in Black II,* the company's sales tripled, amounting to what a company representative claimed was the equivalent of $25 million in free ads.[8]

But since the days of *E.T.* and *Top Gun,* product placement in the movies has grown to levels of near absurdity. When *Die Another Day,* a 2002 installment in the James Bond franchise, managed to display twenty-three brands over the course of 123 minutes, audiences were royally peeved. Most critics questioned the movie's integrity, some even dubbing it *Buy Another Day.* But this was nothing compared to Sylvester Stallone's 2001 *Driven* (which probably would have sparked similar outrage had people actually seen it), which managed to jam in 103 brands in 117 minutes—almost a brand every sixty seconds. More recently, the movie *Transformers* had unannounced cameos from AAA, Apple, Aquafina, AT&T, and Austin-Healey—and those were just the *A*s. All in all, sixty-eight companies made utterly forgettable, face-in-the-crowd appearances in the 2007 film.

These days, we're yanked, tugged, pelted, pushed, prodded, reminded, cajoled, whispered at, overloaded, and overwhelmed by a constant stream of in-your-face product placement. The result? Snow-blindness. Or close to it. By any chance, did you happen to see *Casino Royale,* the latest James Bond movie starring Daniel Craig? Do you remember any products that were featured in the film? FedEx? Bond's Omega Watch? Sony's Vaio computer? Louis Vuitton? Ford? Believe it or not, they all made uncredited walk-ons. Ford, in fact, manufactures every single car in *Casino Royale,* including a Land Rover, a Jaguar, a Lincoln, and Bond's signature Aston Martin. And Sony showcased not just its Vaio computer but its Ericsson phones, Blu-ray players and LCD televisions.[9] But if you're like me, the only product you remember from *Casino*

Royale is the Aston Martin, and that's probably due more to a
well-known association with James Bond cemented over the
years than an actual memory from the movie (and with the
cheapest Aston Martin selling for around $120,000, I doubt
there were all that many takers).

When it comes to product placement, television is hardly
left behind. Leslie Moonves, chairman of the CBS Corporation, predicts that soon up to 75 percent of all scripted prime-
time network shows will feature products and plotlines that
advertisers have paid for.[10] It's a staggeringly high figure that,
if he's right, would further muddy the already-fragile lines between advertising and creative content so profoundly as to
alter the very meaning of entertainment. Rance Crain, the
editor-in-chief of *Advertising Age,* once put it succinctly: "Advertisers will not be satisfied until they put their mark on every
blade of grass."[11]

WE'D PRESENTED OUR brain-scan subjects with a sequence
of twenty product logos, each one appearing for a single second. Some were logos for various companies that aired thirty-
second commercials during *American Idol,* including Coke,
Ford, and Cingular. We called these product placements
branded logos. We also showed our volunteers logos from
companies that had no products placed within the show—
everything from Fanta to Verizon to Target to eBay. We re-
ferred to these as unbranded logos, meaning they had no
connection or sponsorship affiliation with the show. Then we
showed our viewers a twenty-minute-long special edition of
American Idol, as well as an episode of a different show that

would serve as a benchmark to statistically validate our final results. When our viewers had finished watching the two shows, we rescreened the precise same sequence of logos three times in a row.

Our goal was to find out whether viewers would remember which logos they had seen during the show and which ones they hadn't. Over the years, neuromarketing research has found that consumers' memory of a product, whether it's deodorant, perfume, or a brand of tequila, is the most relevant, reliable measure of an ad's effectiveness. It's also linked with subjects' future buying behavior. In other words, if we remember Mitchum Roll-On, Calvin Klein's Euphoria, and Don Julio Anejo tequila, we'll be far more likely to reach for them the next time we're in a store or add them to our cart the next time we're shopping online. So it made sense to compare the strength of subjects' memories for the logos—both Branded and Unbranded—that they'd seen both before and after watching *American Idol*.

A week later, Professor Silberstein and I met up to discuss the results.

First, in the before-the-program testing, Professor Silberstein had found that despite how frequently the products from the three major sponsors—Ford, Cingular Wireless, and Coca-Cola—appeared in *American Idol,* the subjects showed no more memory for these products than for any of the other randomly chosen products they viewed before the study began. Meaning, our branded logos and our unbranded logos began the race on even ground.

It wouldn't stay that way for long. After viewing the programs, subjects showed a significantly greater recall for our branded logos than for unbranded ones. What's more, the sheer potency of the branded logos—the ones that had placed their products strategically throughout the program or advertised during the program—had actually *inhibited* the recall of the unbranded logos. In other words, after watching the two shows, subjects' memories for the branded logos, like Coke and Cingular, had crowded out memories of the unbranded ones, such as Pepsi and Verizon.

But then came the most bizarre, potentially profound finding of all. The SST results showed that Coca-Cola was way more memorable than Cingular Wireless and far, far more memorable than Ford. What was even more amazing was that Ford didn't *just* do poorly. In its post-program test, we discovered that after viewing the shows, our subjects actually remembered *less* about the Ford commercials than they had before they entered the study. Talk about driving away potential customers. In other words, watching the Coke-saturated show actually *suppressed* subjects' memories of the Ford ads. The car company, it appeared, had invested $26 million in yearly sponsorship—and actually *lost* market share.

So why was Coke's strategy so successful, while Ford's wasn't? They both spent the same stupendous amount of money on their media campaigns. They both ran countless commercials during the same program. They both reached the same amount of viewers. What was going on here?

To understand the results, think back to the way in which their advertising was integrated into the program. Coke permeated 60 percent of the show's running time with its artfully placed cups, furniture evoking the shape of its bottles, and Coke-red walls. Ford, on the other hand, simply ran traditional commercials that didn't intrude on the program at all. In other words, Coke was integrated fully into the narrative (company reps might as well have been pouring the stuff over our volunteers' heads), while Ford wasn't at all. For example, you don't see any Ford-shaped couches or logos on the *American Idol* set. Contestants don't drive onstage, or slink offstage, in a Ford. What about a Ford coffee mug? A Ford necktie? A Ford runner-up prize? No such things exist. Despite their $26 million worth of ad spots, Ford, quite simply, doesn't play a role in the show.

In short, the results revealed that we have no memory of brands that don't play an integral part in the storyline of a program. They become white noise, easily, instantaneously forgotten. When we see a commercial showing *Idol* contestants merrily sponging down a Ford at a car wash, or crowding into a vehicle like lunatic 1950s teenagers, we pay practically no attention to the product, because it's clearly "just" an ad.

Through subtle and brilliant integration, Coke, on the other hand, has painstakingly affiliated itself with the dreams, aspirations, and starry-eyed fantasies of potential idols. Want to be high-flying and adored? Coke can help. Want to have the world swooning at your feet? Drink a Coke. By merely sipping the drink onstage, the three judges forged a powerful association between the drink and the emotions provoked by the show. Similarly, Cingular became associated as the instrument through which contestants can either accomplish their dreams or at the very least become a D-list celebrity. Ford, on the other hand, has no such archetypal role whatsoever on *American Idol*. Viewers don't link it with victory, defeat, dreams, adoration, klieg lights, standing ovations, encores—or anything other than gas, tires, highways, and automatic transmissions. *Idol* contestants have no natural connection or aspirational affiliation with the brand so we, as viewers, have no emotional engagement with it, either.

And products that play an integral part in the narrative of a program—like Coke and, to a lesser extent, Cingular Wireless—are not only more memorable, they even appear to have a double-barreled effect. In other words, they not only *increase* our memory of the product, but they actually *weaken* our ability to remember the other brands.

As our SST study showed, for product placement to work, it has to be a lot slyer and more sophisticated than simply plunking a series of random products on a screen and expecting us to respond. Let's revisit *E.T.* for a moment. Elliott didn't just pop those Reese's Pieces into his mouth during a thoughtless bike ride with his buddies; they were an essential part of the storyline because they were used to lure E.T. from the woods. To give another example, many of us who have seen Spielberg's *Minority Report* still recall the witty 2054 animated edition of *USA Today* (with the headline "PreCrime Hunts Its Own," accompanied by a photo of Tom Cruise's head snapping from left to right) that a passenger was reading on a train during a crucial moment in the film. Yet we don't remember the same newspaper when it made fleeting appearances in *Black Hawk Down, Barbershop,* and *Maid in Manhattan.* That's also why in *Casino Royale,* the cameo shots of FedEx, Louis Vuitton, and other product placements were the equivalent of staring at the sky; like the Ford commercials, they had no relevance whatsoever to the plot.

What's more, in order for product placements to work, the product has to *make sense* within the show's narrative. So if a product isn't a good match with the movie or TV show

in which it appears—if the latest Bruce Willis shoot-
'em-up movie has product placements, say, for cotton swabs,
strawberry-flavored dental floss, or the Body Shop's new
scented lotion—viewers will tune it right out. But if the same
movie features a scene of our hero at the gym mastering a
new brand of exercise equipment or downing a Molson before he takes on two bullies in an alleyway single-handedly,
viewers will respond more positively. Which is why, in the future, consumers are unlikely to see product placements for
power saws, tractor-trailers, or Hummer RVs in the latest
Reese Witherspoon film.

In other words, advertisers and marketers who blizzard us
with brand after brand—a Mountain Dew and a Dell laptop
here, a GNC super vitamin and a Posturepedic mattress
there—might as well light a match to the millions of dollars
they've spent on their ads. Unless the brand in question plays
a fundamental part of the storyline, we won't remember it, period. And therein lies Ford's multimillion-dollar mistake.

But what exactly is it in our brains that makes some products so much more memorable and appealing than others?
Well, we're about to take a look at one of the most fascinating
brain discoveries of recent times, one that plays an enormous
role in why we're attracted to the things we are. The place:
Parma, Italy. The unwitting codiscoverers of this phenomenon? A species of monkey known as the macaque.

3

I'LL HAVE WHAT
SHE'S HAVING

Mirror Neurons at Work

IN 2004, STEVE JOBS,
CEO, chairman, and co-founder of Apple, was strolling along
Madison Avenue in New York City when he noticed something strange, and gratifying. Hip white earphones (remember,
back then most earphones came in basic boring black). Loop-
ing and snaking out of people's ears, dangling down across
their chests, peeking out of pockets and purses and backpacks.
They were everywhere. "It was, like, on every block, there was
someone with white headphones, and I thought, 'Oh, my God,
it's starting to happen,'" Jobs, who'd recently launched his
company's immensely successful iPod, was quoted as saying.[1]

You could term the popularity of the iPod (and its ubiquitous, iconic white headphones) a fad. Some might even call it
a revolution. But from a neuroscientific point of view, what
Jobs was seeing was nothing less than the triumph of a region
of our brains associated with something called the mirror
neuron.

In 1992, an Italian scientist named Giacomo Rizzolatti and

his research team in Parma, Italy, were studying the brains of a species of monkey—the macaque—in the hopes of finding out how the brain organizes motor behaviors. Specifically, they were looking at a region of the macaque brain known by neuroscientists as F5, or the premotor area, which registers activity when monkeys carry out certain gestures, like picking up a nut. Interestingly, they observed that the macaques' premotor neurons would light up not just when the monkeys reached for that nut, but also when they saw *other* monkeys reaching for a nut—which came as a surprise to Rizzolatti's team, since neurons in premotor regions of the brain typically don't respond to visual stimulation.

On one particularly hot summer afternoon, Rizzolatti and his team observed the strangest thing of all when one of Dr. Rizzolatti's grad students returned to the lab after lunch holding an ice cream cone, and noticed that the macaque was staring at him, almost longingly. And as the grad student raised the cone to his mouth and took a tentative lick, the electronic monitor hooked up to the macaque's premotor region fired— *bripp, bripp, bripp.*

The monkey hadn't done a thing. It hadn't moved its arm or taken a lick of ice cream; it wasn't even holding anything at all. But simply by *observing* the student bringing the ice cream cone to his mouth, the monkey's brain had mentally imitated the very same gesture.

This amazing phenomenon was what Rizzolatti would eventually dub "mirror neurons" at work—neurons that fire when an action is being performed and when that same action is being observed. "It took us several years to believe what we were seeing," he later said.

But the monkeys' mirror neurons didn't fire up at the sight

of just *any* gesture either a grad student or another monkey made. Rizzolatti's team was able to demonstrate that the macaques' mirror neurons were responding to what are known as "targeted gestures"—meaning those activities that involve an object, such as picking up a nut, or bringing an ice cream cone to your mouth, as opposed to random movement, such as crossing the room or simply standing there with your arms crossed.

Do humans' brains work in the same way? Do we, too, mimic how others interact with objects? Well, for obvious ethical reasons scientists can't place an electrode into a working human brain. However, fMRI and EEG scans of the regions of the human brain thought to contain mirror neurons, the inferior frontal cortex and superior parietal lobule, point to yes, as these regions are activated both when someone is performing an action, as well as when the person observes another person performing an action. The evidence supporting the existence of mirror neurons in the human brain is so compelling, in fact, that one eminent professor of psychology and neuroscience at the University of California has said, "What DNA is for biology, the Mirror Neuron is for psychology."[2]

Have you ever wondered why, when you're watching a baseball game and your favorite player strikes out in the top of the ninth inning, you cringe—or alternately, why, when your home team scores a goal or a touchdown, you pump your arm in the air? Or why, when you're at the movies and the heroine starts weeping, tears well up in your own eyes? What about that rush of exhilaration you feel when Clint Eastwood or Vin Diesel dispatches a villain—or that alpha-male stride-in-your-step you still feel an hour after the movie ends? Or the feeling of grace and beauty that floods through you as you observe a ballet dancer or listen to a world-class pianist? Chalk it up to mirror neurons. Just like Rizzolatti's monkeys, when we watch someone do something, whether it's scoring a penalty kick or playing a perfect arpeggio on a Steinway grand piano, our brains react as if we were actually performing these activities ourselves. In short, it's as though seeing and doing are one and the same.

Mirror neurons are also responsible for why we often unwittingly imitate other people's behavior. This tendency is so innate it can even be observed in babies—just stick your tongue out at a baby, and the baby will very likely repeat the action. When other people whisper, we tend to lower our own voices. When we're around an older person, we're prone to walking more slowly. If we're seated on an airplane next to someone with a pronounced accent, many of us unconsciously begin to imitate it. I can remember visiting in Moscow back in the cold war days, and being struck that there were no colors anywhere in the city. The sky was gray, the houses were gray, the cars were gray, and the faces of the people I passed on the streets were unrelentingly pale. But what really stood out for me the most was that virtually no one was smiling. As I walked along, I'd give the other pedestrians in Moscow a quick smile of acknowledgment, and time and again, I'd get back nothing in return. At first, this was amusing (because it was so strange), but after about an hour, I started to realize the effect it was having on me. My mood changed. I wasn't feeling my usual lighthearted self. I'd quit smiling. I felt borderline grim. I felt *gray*. Physically and psychologically, without even realizing it, I'd been mirroring everyone else around me.

Mirror neurons explain why we often smile when we see someone who is happy or wince when we see someone who is in physical pain. Scientist Tania Singer scanned subjects' brains as they watched another person experience physical pain, and found that those subjects' "pain-related" regions—including the fronto-insular and anterior cingulated cortices—came alive. It seemed that by the mere observation of another person's pain, these subjects felt the pain as if it were their own.

Interestingly, mirror neurons are also at work when the opposite takes place—on those occasions when, in what is known as schadenfreude, we actually take pleasure in others' bad luck. Singer and her colleagues showed volunteers a clip of people playing a game. Some players cheated; others played fairly, by the rules. Next, the volunteers looked on as some of the players—both the cheaters and the noncheaters—were given a mild but painful electric shock.[3]

Thanks to mirror neurons, the pain-related regions in both the male and female brains lit up in empathy when the noncheaters` experienced the shock. But when the cheaters were shocked, the male subjects' brains not only showed less empathy, their reward centers actually lit up (the women in the group still maintained a noticeable level of empathy). In other words, we all tend to empathize when bad things happen to good people—in this case the noncheaters—but when bad things happen to bad people—the cheaters—men, at least, actually experience a degree of pleasure.

Yawn. Are you yawning now, or feeling the initial stirrings of yawning? I am, and not because I'm bored, or tired of writing about the brain, but simply because I just typed the word

Yawn. You see, mirror neurons become activated not only when we're *observing* other people's behavior, they even fire when we're *reading* about someone performing it.

Recently, a team of researchers at UCLA used an fMRI to scan subjects' brains while they read phrases that described a host of actions like "biting the peach" and "grasping a pen." Later, when the same subjects observed videos of people performing these same two simple actions, the identical cortical regions of the brains lit up.[4] If I simply write the words "nails scratching on a chalkboard" or "sucking on a lemon" or "giant hairy black widow spider," chances are good that you'll wince, recoil, and otherwise squirm while reading them (your mind visualizes that painful sound, the bitter taste of the lemon wedge, those furry legs edging along your calf). Those are your mirror neurons at work. Unilever executives told me once that during a focus group they were conducting on a new shampoo, they noticed consumers would begin scratching their heads whenever a member of the team said the word *scratch* or *scratching*. Mirror neurons again. According to the results of one fMRI study, "When we read a book, these specialized cells respond as if we are actually doing what the book character is doing."[5]

In short, everything we observe (or read about) someone else doing, we do as well—in our minds. If you saw me tripping and falling headfirst down a flight of stairs, your mirror neurons would fire up, and you would know precisely how I feel (even though you're not half as clumsy as I am). Thus mirror neurons not only help us imitate other people, they're responsible for human empathy. They send signals to the limbic system, or emotional region, of our brains—the area that helps us tune in to one another's feelings and responses—so we can experience what it's like to walk—or in this case, trip and sprawl—in another person's shoes.

WHAT STEVE JOBS observed on that New York City day was a good example of mirror neurons in our everyday lives—and the role they play in why we buy. Just as mirror neurons caused those monkeys' brains to mentally imitate the grad student's motion, so do they make us humans mimic each other's buying behavior. So when we see a pair of unusual earphones sticking out of someone else's ears, our mirror neurons trigger a desire in us to have those same cool-looking accessories, too. But it goes deeper than simple desire.

To see this in action, let's pay a quick visit to the mall. Imagine that you're a woman passing the front window of the Gap. A shapely mannequin wearing hip-hugging, perfectly worn-in jeans, a simple summery white blouse, and a red bandanna stops you in your tracks. She looks great—slim, sexy, confident, relaxed, and appealing. Subconsciously, even though you've put on a few pounds, you think, *I could look like that, too, if I just bought that outfit. I could be her. In those clothes, I, too, could have her freshness, her youthful nonchalance.* At least that's what your brain is telling you, whether you're aware of it or not. Next thing you know, you march into the Gap, whip out your Visa, and stroll out fifteen minutes later with the jeans, blouse, and bandanna under your arm. It's as though you've just bought an image, an attitude, or both. Or, let's imagine you're a bachelor hitting up Best Buy. After browsing the 52-

inch HDTV section, you try out a popular new game for the Nintendo Wii called Guitar Hero 3: Legends of Rock, which allows players to strap the plastic guitar around their neck and play along to songs like Cream's "Sunshine of Your Love," Pearl Jam's "Even Flow," and the Stones' "Paint It Black." You've always wanted to be a rock star—your thirty-year-old Fender is at home collecting dust—and this is a quick and dirty way to achieve your fantasy. Though it's only a game, you feel what it must be like to be Jagger, or Clapton, or Eddie Vedder, and, not surprisingly, you end up buying one.

Just as that woman's brain let her experience what it feels like to look like that Gap mannequin, this man's brain told him what it would feel like to live out his rock 'n' roll dreams. In both cases, their mirror neurons overrode their rational thinking and caused them to unconsciously imitate—and purchase—what was in front of them.

And that's just how our mirror neurons work on us as consumers. Think about how *other* people's behavior affects our shopping experience, and ultimately influences our purchasing decisions. Take smiling, for example. Two researchers recently created what they called the Smiling Study—a look at how joy, or happiness, affects shoppers. They asked fifty-five volunteers to imagine that they'd just entered an imaginary travel agency. Once there, they had to interact with one of three people: a smiling woman, a woman who looked despondent, and a woman who seemed completely fed up. Which of the volunteers do you think reported the more positive (imaginary) experience? You guessed it, those who interacted with the smiling agent. The study revealed that a smiling face "evokes more joy in the target person than a non-smiling face," and that it also produces a far more positive overall attitude toward the business in question. Not only that, the volunteers who imagined interacting with the smiling person reported that they would be more likely to keep on patronizing the company in question.[6]

According to Duke University researchers, we're not only attracted to people who smile but we also tend to remember their names. In a 2008 fMRI study, Professors Takashi Tsukiura and Roberto Cabeza showed subjects pictures of smiling and unsmiling individuals, followed by their names, e.g. "Nancy," "Amber," "Kristy," and so on. The results found that the subjects' orbitofrontal cortices—the region of the brain associated with reward processing—were more active when the subjects were learning and recalling the names of smiling individuals. "We are sensitive to positive social signals," Cabeza explained. "We want to remember people who were kind to us, in case we interact with them in the future."[7]

Mirror neurons can even respond to things we see online. Take the case of a Detroit, Michigan, seventeen-year-old named Nick Baily. On November 6, 2006, Nintendo released its highly anticipated Wii gaming system—the machine that allows players to simulate the swing of a bat, the arc of a tennis serve, the roll of a bowling ball, or the rush of a linebacker crashing into the end zone via a hand-held remote. After seventeen hours waiting in line at his local Toys "R" Us, the high school senior rushed excitedly home, his Wii box tucked under one arm.

Now, most new Wii owners would breathlessly tear open the box, hook up the machine to the TV set, and test out the new gadget right away before the dust at their heels had time to settle. Not Nick Baily. Before opening the container, he set up his video camera, clipped a microphone to his shirt lapel, adjusted the video camera's controls, and pressed record. Only then, with the video rolling, did he begin unsealing his Wii.

A couple of hours later, Nick's very own grand opening could be viewed on YouTube—and it was, approximately 71,000 times in the first week alone. It seemed that simply watching someone else enjoying the unveiling of a new Wii gave Nintendo fans out there almost as much pleasure as opening that new Wii themselves. In fact, there are entire video-sharing sites devoted to this kind of vicarious pleasure; on www.unbox.it.com and www.unboxing.com, computer users can watch strangers from all across the world slit or scissor open their various purchases. As Chad Stoller, executive director of Emerging Platforms at the ad agency Organic, explains, "It's the culmination of lust. There are a lot of people who aspire, who want to have something they may not be able to afford, and they can't buy it yet. They are looking for some way to satiate their appetite." Or maybe it's just mirror neurons at work.

This concept of imitation is a huge factor in why we buy the things we do. Have you ever been disinterested in, or even repulsed by, a certain product, then after time, changed your mind? Maybe it's a style of shoe you thought was hideous (say, Crocs) until you started seeing it on every third pair of feet you passed. Suddenly, you went from "Those are ugly" to "I have to have those—now." My point is, sometimes just seeing a certain product over and over makes it more desirable. We see models in fashion magazines and we want to dress like them or make up our faces the way they do. We watch the rich and famous driving expensive cars and cavorting in their lavishly decorated homes and think, *I want to live like that.* We see

our friend's snazzy new LCD TV, or Bang & Olufsen tele-
phone, and by God, we want one for ourselves.

But mirror neurons don't work alone. Often, they work in
tandem with dopamine, one of the brain's pleasure chemicals.
Dopamine is one of the most addictive substances known to
man—and purchasing decisions are driven in some part by its
seductive effects. When you see that shiny digital camera, or
those flashy diamond earrings, for example, dopamine subtly
flushes your brain with pleasure, then wham, before you know
it, you've signed the credit card receipt (researchers generally
agree that it takes as little as 2.5 seconds to make a purchasing
decision).[8] A few minutes later, as you exit the store, bag in
hand, the euphoric feelings caused by the dopamine recede,
and all of a sudden you wonder whether you'll really ever use
that damn camera or wear those earrings. Sound familiar?

Surely we've all heard the term "retail therapy." And as we
all know, whether our vice is shoes, CDs, or electronics, shopping can be addictive. If nothing else, shopping—for anything
from Twinkies to Maytag refrigerators to Bulgari watches—
has become an enormous part of what we do in our spare
time. But does it actually make us happier? All scientific indi-
cators point to *yes*—at least in the very short term. And that
dose of happiness can be attributed to dopamine, the brain's
flush of reward, pleasure and well-being. When we first decide
to buy something, the brain cells that release dopamine secrete
a burst of good feeling, and this dopamine rush fuels our instinct to keep shopping even when our rational minds tell us
we've had enough. As Professor David Laibson, an economist
at Harvard University, puts it, "Our emotional brain wants to
max out the credit card, even though our logical brain knows
we should save for retirement."[9]

This phenomenon, believe it or not, can be traced way back to our age-old instinct for survival. As UCLA's Dr. Susan Brookheimer points out, "Dopamine activity in the brain increases in anticipation of many different types of rewards, from gambling-related rewards to monetary to social rewards."[10] In other words, that crazy rush of pleasure we may experience from the anticipation of buying, say, a new Black-Berry or Nano may actually be helping us enhance our reproductive success and preparing us for survival. Why? Because consciously or not, we calculate purchases based on how they might bring us social status—and status is linked with reproductive success.

In fact, scientists have found that an area in the frontal cortex of the brain called Brodmann area 10, which is activated when we see products we think are "cool" (as opposed to, say, an old Ford Fairlane, or a set of new lug wrenches), is associated with self-perception and social emotions. In other words, whether we know it or not, we assess snazzy stuff—iPhones, Harleys, and such—largely in terms of their capacity to enhance our social status. So that slinky new Prada dress or that shiny new Alfa Romeo might be just what we need to attract a mate who could possibly end up carrying on our genetic line or providing for us for life.[11]

What's the connection, then, between dopamine and mirror neurons? Let's watch our brains in action as we pay a visit to Abercrombie & Fitch, the clothing mecca for tweens and teens. In many of its stores, especially those in large urban cities, the company positions large blow-up posters of half-naked models just inside their doors. Not only that, they hire actual models to hang out in front of the store in groups. Naturally, both the poster and the real-life models are all attired in

form-fitting Abercrombie clothes (at least those who are wearing much of anything), and they look fantastic—young, sexy,
healthy, and preposterously good-looking. Clearly, they're
members of the hip, popular crowd (at the Abercrombie's
Fifth Avenue store in New York, you'll notice that tens if not
hundreds of pedestrians will slow down and linger in their
vicinity). Let's say you're a socially uncertain fourteen-year-old.
As you pass by the store, your mirror neurons fire up. You can
imagine yourself among them: popular, desired, at the center
of it all.

Then—you just can't help it—you go into the store. The
place is designed to resemble a dark, noisy nightclub, and the
people working there are just as sinuous and good-looking as
the models on the billboard and the models milling around on
the sidewalk outside. One of the salesgirls asks if she can help
you. *Help me?* your brain echoes. *Damn straight—you can help me*
become *you.* You inhale that cloying, characteristic Abercrombie fragrance that lingers in your nostrils long after you've left
the store—and before you've even tried on a single item of
clothing, your brain is sold.

You approach the counter with the clothing you've just
picked out. As you're getting ready to blow a bundle on jeans
and sweaters, your dopamine level soars into the stratosphere.
As the clerk rings up and bags your purchases in that beautiful
black-and-white Abercrombie bag tattooed with bare-chested
models, you're feeling cool, you're feeling gorgeous—you're
feeling like one of "them." Which produces a feeling the brain
automatically links back to the models outside, the fragrant
and pervasive smell, and the late-night atmosphere of the store
itself—and when you tuck that gorgeous bag under your arm,
you're taking home a little bit of that popularity with you.

A few days later, you're walking down the street when you spy another Abercrombie store. Actually, the smell hits you first, from a hundred yards away—and instantaneously brings back to you that dopamine rush you experienced when you were last inside. Again, your mirror neurons take in the scantily clad models adorning the store entrance, and the paid models idling outside, and irresistibly, as if yanked by a silver thread, you're drawn back inside to get another shot of pleasure and reward—and another charge to your parents' credit card. Between your mirror neurons making you feel sexy and attractive, and your dopamine creating that near-orgasmic anticipation of reward, your rational mind doesn't stand a chance.

As we saw, video games like Guitar Hero 3, computer games such as "The Sims," and virtual Web sites like Second Life also owe their popularity in large part to mirror neurons. Whether we've mastered a complicated riff on Guitar Hero, or purchased a shiny new Beamer on Second Life, our mirror neurons help us connect emotionally to these virtual realities. So even if we're sitting in a dark, subterranean basement in front of a glowing screen, these games offer us a virtual means of experiencing the same rush of pleasure we would feel if we were living these fantasies and dreams in our actual lives.

Now we know why actors who smoke on screen make us want to reach for our packs, or start smoking in the first place (half of teen smokers may begin their habit thanks to smoking in movies—390,000 each year); why stick-thin models have caused a fearsome jump in anorexia among young girls; why just about every man in the universe can quote Michael Corleone in *The Godfather*; why the dance craze the Macarena spread; and why when Michael Jackson moonwalked for the first time, we all felt his kineticism in our own veins—then rushed out to buy *Thriller*. (Along with a single white glove—which became a major merchandising phenomenon.) And I predict that in the future, as marketers begin to learn more about how mirror neurons drive our behavior, they'll find more and more ways to play upon them to get us to buy.

So buyers beware. Because the future of advertising isn't smoke and mirrors—it's mirror neurons. And they will prove even more powerful in driving our loyalty, our minds, our wallets, and our Buyology than even the marketers themselves could have anticipated.

How? Well, to find out, we're first going to travel across the Atlantic to a brain-scanning lab in a university town in central England. We're going to revisit cigarettes and the subject of craving, and look at how subliminal signals assaulting us from billboards, store shelves, and maybe even our own living room can cause us to buy. And be warned: what we're about to see (or rather, not see) may shock you.

4

Subliminal Messaging,
Alive and Well

IT WAS THE SUMMER OF 1957. Dwight D. Eisenhower had begun his second term in office, Elvis had made his last appearance on the *Ed Sullivan Show*, Jack Kerouac's *On the Road* debuted in bookstores, and over a six-week period, 45,699 moviegoers crowded inside the movie theater in Fort Lee, New Jersey, to watch William Holden as an ex-jock-turned-drifter fall for Kim Novak, a Kansas girl who's already spoken for, in the cinematic version of William Inge's play *Picnic*.

But unbeknownst to audiences, this version of *Picnic* had an apparently sinister twist. It turns out that a market researcher by the name of James Vicary had placed a mechanical slide projector in the screening room, and had projected the words "Drink Coca-Cola" and "Eat Popcorn" for a duration of $\frac{1}{3000}$ of a second onscreen every five seconds during every showing of the movie.

Vicary, who is famous to this day for coining the term *subliminal advertising,* claimed that during his experiment, the Fort

Lee theater saw an 18.1 percent increase in Coca-Cola sales and a whopping 57.8 percent surge in popcorn purchases, all thanks to the suggestive powers of his hidden messages.

The experiment touched a nerve in an American public already jumpy from cold war paranoia and inflamed by the publication of Vance Packard's book *The Hidden Persuaders*, which exposed the psychologically manipulative methods marketers were bringing to advertising. Consumers were convinced that the government could use the same kinds of under-the-radar techniques to peddle propaganda, that the Communists could use them to recruit supporters, or that cults could use them to brainwash members. As a result, American television networks and the National Association of Broadcasters banned subliminal ads in June of 1958.

In 1962, Dr. Henry Link, the president of the Psychological Corporation, challenged Vicary to repeat his Coke-and-popcorn test. Yet this time the experiment yielded no jump whatsoever in either Coke or popcorn sales. In an interview with *Advertising Age*, Vicary came out and somewhat puzzlingly admitted that his experiment was a gimmick—he'd made the whole thing up. The mechanical slide projector, the surge in popcorn and Coca-Cola sales—none of it was true. Despite Vicary's confession, the damage was done, and a belief in the power of subliminal messaging had been firmly planted in the American public's mind.

Shortly thereafter, the American Psychological Association pronounced subliminal advertising "confused, ambiguous and not as effective as traditional advertising," and the issue—and the ban—appeared to be laid to rest.[1] Predictably, consumer paranoia about the topic drifted away, just as it would time and again over the next half-century as consumers and advocacy groups occasionally petitioned for stricter laws, only to have governmental agencies fail to pass any outright federal legislation.

But then, some fifteen years after Vicary's faux-experiment, Dr. Wilson B. Key published his book *Subliminal Seduction* with a cover photograph picturing a cocktail with a lemon wedge in it, accompanied by the irresistible teaser, *Are you being sexually aroused by this picture?* Soon, a new wave of paranoia burbled through the country. This time around, the FCC announced in January 1974 that subliminal techniques in advertising, whether they worked or not, were "contrary to the public interest," and therefore, any station using them was in danger of losing its broadcast license.[2]

Still, today, there are no explicit bans against subliminal advertising in the United States or the United Kingdom, though the Federal Trade Commission has taken the official position that a subliminal ad "that causes consumers to unconsciously select certain goods or services, or to alter their normal behavior, might constitute a deceptive or unfair practice."[3] The emphasis here is on *might*—to this day, no official regulations or guidelines as to what constitutes subliminal advertising exist.

Generally speaking, subliminal messages are defined as visual, auditory, or any other sensory messages that register just below our level of conscious perception and can be detected only by the subconscious mind. But despite the hype and worry that have surrounded subliminal advertising over the past half century, the topic tends to be treated with good-natured eye-rolling. *Who do they think they're fooling?* is how most of us react whenever a story about subliminal advertising shows up on the news, whether it's a report of a McDonald's logo flashing for ⅟₃₀ of a second during the Food Channel's *Iron Chef America* program (a spokesperson for the Food Channel claimed it was a technical error), or an unfounded rumor that a cloud of dust in Disney's *The Lion King* spells out "s-e-x."

Still, accusations of subliminal messages do crop up from time to time, especially in the movies. In 1973, during a showing of *The Exorcist,* one petrified moviegoer fainted and broke his jaw on the seat in front of him. He sued Warner Brothers, and the filmmakers, claiming that the subliminal images of a demon's face flashed throughout the movie had caused him to pass out.[4] And in 1999, some viewers accused the makers of the film *Fight Club* of subliminal manipulation, claiming they had planted pornographic images of Brad Pitt in the movie in a deliberate attempt, according to one Web site, to enhance the film's "anti-work message and revolutionary tone."

Accusations of subliminal manipulation have been leveled at musicians from Led Zeppelin (play "Stairway to Heaven" backward and you'll supposedly hear "Oh, here's to my sweet Satan") to Queen ("Another One Bites the Dust" played backward allegedly yields "It's fun to smoke marijuana").

And in 1990, the parents of two eighteen-year-old boys from Nevada who had attempted suicide took the British heavy-metal band Judas Priest to court, charging that the band had inserted subliminal messages—including "Let's be dead" and "Do it"—inside its song lyrics. Though both boys were high school dropouts from severely troubled families, one of the boys who survived the joint suicide attempt was later quoted in a letter as saying, "I believe that alcohol and heavy-metal music such as Judas Priest led us to be mesmerized."[5] The suit was later dismissed.

Much of the time, when subliminal messages show up in

our culture, they're selling sex. Take the 1995 Yellow Pages advertisement for an English flooring company called D.J. Flooring, whose motto is "Laid by the Best." When held upright, this ad features an image of a woman holding a champagne glass, but tip it over, and what you see is an image of a woman masturbating. In a montage of print ads someone showed me once, I saw an ad for an exercise machine that showed a bare-chested young man with rippling abs on which were imprinted—or was I, and everybody else, imagining it?—the silhouette of an erect penis. A second ad, for a ketchup company, featured a hot dog and, poised over it, a dollop of ketchup coming out of a bottle that resembled a human tongue. And a recent example shows a woman with her manicured fingers resting on a computer mouse that rather uncannily suggests a clitoris.

In 1990, Pepsi was asked to withdraw one of its specially designed "Cool Can" designs from the market when a consumer complained that when the six-packs were stacked a certain way on a shelf, they produced a pattern spelling out s-e-x. A Pepsi advertising manager denied any ulterior motive, saying only, "The cans were designed to be cool and fun and different; something to get the customer's attention," while a Pepsi spokesman insisted that the message was an "odd coincidence."[6] Sure was.

But not all subliminal messaging is as subtle. Today, some stores play tapes of jazz or Latino music (available through more than one Web site) that conceal recorded messages—imperceptible to our conscious minds—designed to prod shoppers into spending more or to discourage shoplifting. Among the messages: "Don't worry about the money," and "Imagine owning it," and "Don't take it, you'll get caught."

According to one vendor, in stores that broadcast these tapes overall sales are up 15 percent, while store thefts have fallen by 58 percent.

And if, as I've long believed, subliminal advertising can be understood as subconscious messages conveyed by advertisers in an attempt to attract us to a product, then it is even more prevalent than anyone has ever realized. After all, in today's overstimulated world, countless things slip beneath our conscious radar every day. Consider the Gershwin standard that plays in the clothing store while we're shopping for a swanky new summer suit—sure, we can hear it, but we're too distracted to consciously register the fact that it's playing. Or what about the small print on a snazzy product package—it's right in front of our eyes, but we're too overstimulated by all the bright colors, fancy typography, and witty copy to actually read it. Or what about the aromas that are pumped into casinos, airplane cabins, hotel rooms, and just-off-the-assembly-line cars? (I hate to tell you this, but the seductively leathery smell of a new car comes out of an aerosol can.) Aren't these essentially subliminal messages? Couldn't it even be argued that with so many TV commercials, magazine ads, and Internet pop-ups constantly demanding our attention, these messages too have become subliminal, in the sense that we *almost* register them, but not really?

Then there are those advertisers who openly use subliminal advertising. In 2006, KFC ran an ad for its Buffalo Snacker chicken sandwich that, if the viewer replayed it in slow motion, revealed a code that consumers could enter on the KFC Web site to receive a coupon for a free Snacker. Though ostensibly aimed at countering a rise in ad-skipping technologies such as TiVo by giving viewers an incentive to actually watch the commercial, KFC was nevertheless using hidden messages (if the commercial was played at normal speed, the codes weren't consciously perceptible) to promote their product.[7] Other advertisers have found a way to make split-second impressions work, but don't call them "subliminal" anymore. By the 1990s, they'd taken on a new name: "primes" or "visual drumbeats." In 2006, Clear Channel Communications introduced "blinks," radio ads that last about two seconds, on their commercial radio network. For a blink advertising *The Simpsons,* for example, listeners hear Homer yelling "Woo-Hoo!" against the show's theme music before an announcer breaks in: "Tonight on Fox."

And if political candidates have become brands (which I believe), then subliminal advertising, or priming, is even alive and well in political messaging. One recent example is a 2000 ad produced by the Republican National Committee in which George W. Bush criticizes Al Gore's prescription drug plan for senior citizens. Its tagline: "The Gore prescription plan: Bureaucrats decide." Then, toward the end of the ad, the word *rats* flashes in oversized letters for a split second while an off-screen voice reiterates the phrase, "Bureaucrats decide." The Bush campaign claimed that the ad's producer must have accidentally "botched the hyphenation of 'Bureaucrats,' placing 'Bureauc' and 'rats' in different frames."[8] George W. Bush dismissed the controversy as "weird and bizarre," but after claiming it was "purely accidental," its creator, Alex Castellanos, later confessed that the word *rats* was a visual "drumbeat designed to make you look at the word 'bureaucrats.' "[9]

Then, in 2006, there was the Harold Ford incident. Ford, a light-skinned black man, was running a close senate race in Tennessee against white Republican Bob Corker. In what could only be interpreted as an explicit—if subliminal—attack on Ford's race, Corker and the Republican National Committee produced an ad in which every time the narrator talked about Ford, African tom-tom drums beat, just barely audibly, in the background. The kicker lay in the final words: "Harold Ford: He's Just Not Right." One could infer that what the Republican National Committee actually meant was "he's just not white."

Clearly, subliminal advertising pervades many aspects of our culture and assaults us each and every day. But does it actually exert any influence on our behavior, or does it, like most product placements, get essentially ignored by our brains? That's what the next part of my study would find out.

IN 1999, HARVARD University researchers tested the power of subliminal suggestions on forty-seven people from sixty to eighty-five years old. The researchers flashed a series of words on a screen for a few thousandths of a second while the subjects played a computer game that they were told measured the relationship between their physical and mental skills. One group of seniors was exposed to positive words, including *wise, astute,* and *accomplished.* The other group was given words like *senile, dependent,* and *diseased.* The purpose of this experiment was to see whether exposing elderly people to subliminal messages that suggested stereotypes about aging could affect their behavior, specifically, how well they walked.

The Harvard team then measured the subjects' walking speed and so-called "swing time" (the time they spent with one foot off the ground), and found that, according to the lead researcher, Harvard professor of medicine Jeffrey Haus-dorff, "The gait of those exposed to positive words improved by almost 10 percent." In other words, it seemed that the positive stereotypes had had a positive psychological effect on the subjects, which in turn improved their physical performance. There seemed to be positive evidence that the subliminal suggestions could affect people's behavior.

Subliminal messaging has even been shown to influence how much we are willing to pay for a product. Recently, two researchers demonstrated that brief exposure to images of smiling or frowning faces for sixteen milliseconds—not long enough for volunteers to consciously register the image or identify the emotion—affected the amount of money test subjects were willing to pay for a beverage. When subjects saw flashes of smiling faces, they poured significantly more drink from a pitcher—and were willing to pay twice as much for it—than when they viewed the angry faces. The researchers termed this effect "unconscious emotion," meaning that a minute emotional change had taken place without the subjects being aware of either the stimulus that caused it or any shift in their emotional states. In other words, smiling faces can subconsciously get us to buy more stuff, suggesting that store managers who instruct their employees to smile are on the right track.[10]

Or consider this: the origin of a product may even subconsciously influence how likely we are to buy it. Recently, I was called to Germany to help a struggling perfume brand regain its footing in the market. When I glanced at the bottle to see where the fragrance was manufactured, I noted that instead of the typical glamorous cities (New York, London,

Paris) most perfume-makers print on their canisters, the company had listed decidedly less glamorous ones. Now, Düsseldorf and Oberkochen may be fantastic places to live, but most consumers don't associate them with sophistication, sensuality, or any other swanky qualities we look for in a fragrance. Among other things, I convinced the company to replace those cities with ones we all dream about taking long, bewitching vacations in (we weren't lying; the company *did* have offices in Paris, London, New York, and Rome)—and sales shot up almost instantly.

But the power of subliminal advertising has little to do with the product itself. Instead, it lies in our own brains. In 2005, a University of Pennsylvania postdoctoral student by the name of Sean Polyn used fMRI to study the ways in which the brain hunts down specific memories. Volunteers were shown approximately ninety images in three separate categories: famous faces (Halle Berry, Jack Nicholson), well-known places (e.g., the Taj Mahal), and common everyday objects (such as nail clippers). As the subjects' brains registered the assortment of images, Polyn asked them to place the image in question in a distinguishing mental context. For example, did they love or loathe Jack Nicholson? Would they ever be remotely interested in paying a visit to the Taj Mahal?

A short time later, Polyn asked the volunteers to recall the images. As the subjects' brains scrambled to retrieve them, they exhibited the precise same pattern of brain activity that was present when their brains had first formed the impression. In fact, Polyn and his team found evidence that the subjects were able to recall what category—celebrities, famous places, everyday items—the image was in before they could even recall the name of the image, suggesting that the human brain is capable of recalling images before those images register in our consciousness.

But even if the brain can summon information that lies beneath our level of consciousness, does that mean that this information necessarily informs our behavior? That's what the next brain scan experiment would help us find out. Our subjects were, once again, twenty smokers from the United Kingdom. But this time around, we were looking at more than warning labels. This cigarette-related investigation posed questions about subliminal messaging I'd always wanted to get to the bottom of: Are smokers affected by imagery that lies beneath their level of consciousness? Can cigarette cravings be triggered by images tied to a brand of cigarette but not explicitly linked to smoking—say, the sight of a Marlboro-red Ferrari or a camel riding off into a mountainous sunset? Do smokers even need to read the words *Marlboro* or *Camel* for their brains' craving spots to compel them to tear open a cigarette pack? Is subliminal advertising, those secretly embedded messages designed to appeal to our dreams, fears, wants, and desires, at all effective in stimulating our interest in a product or compelling us to buy?

BUT BEFORE WE get to our fMRI test and its startling results, let's do a little mind experiment of our own. Imagine that you've just walked into a chic urban bar where the clientele is young, good-looking, and hip, where the drinks have exotic names like the Flirtini, and the food is gorgeously minimalist and costs an arm and a leg. As you enter, you briefly take note of the stylish upholstery in a familiar shade of red covering the chairs and couches, but your friend is waving to you from across the room, loud music is playing, and as you try to navigate through the crowds, your eyes firmly fixated on the delicious-looking cocktail beckoning you from the bar, those conscious impressions of your surroundings are soon forgotten.

Strangely enough, you suddenly feel the urge to smoke a Marlboro, although you're not sure why.

Coincidence? Hardly. Thanks to worldwide bans on tobacco advertising on television, in magazines, and just about everywhere else, cigarette companies including Philip Morris, which manufactures Marlboro, and the R.J. Reynolds Tobacco Company, which owns Camel, funnel a huge percentage of their marketing budget into this kind of subliminal brand exposure. Philip Morris, for example, offers bar owners financial incentives to fill their venues with color schemes, specially designed furniture, ashtrays, suggestive tiles designed in captivating shapes similar to parts of the Marlboro logo, and other subtle symbols that, when combined, convey the very essence of Marlboro—without even the mention of the brand name or the sight of an actual logo. These "installations," or "Marlboro Motels" as they're known in the business, usually consist of lounge areas filled with comfy Marlboro red sofas positioned in front of TV screens spooling scenes of the Wild West—with its rugged cowboys, galloping horses, wide open spaces, and red sunsets all designed to evoke the essence of the iconic "Marlboro Man."

To ensure the greatest possible exposure for its product, Marlboro also markets rugged, collectible outdoor cowboy clothing, including gloves, watches, caps, scarves, boots, vests, jackets, and jeans all designed to evoke associations with the brand. The Dunhill store in London sells leather goods, time-pieces, menswear, accessories, and even a fragrance meant to underscore the luxurious image of the brand. In Malaysia, Benson & Hedges has even sponsored brand-themed coffee shops selling products emblazoned with the cigarette's gold logo. As the manager of one of these Kuala Lumpur cafés put it: "The idea is to be smoker-friendly. Smokers associate cof-fee with cigarettes. They are both drugs of a type."[11]

Donna Sturgess, the global head of innovation for the con-sumer business of GlaxoSmithKline, sums up this phenome-non neatly: "It's an unfortunate irony that as a result of government bans, tobacco companies have fast-forwarded into the future—and moved into alternative media, methods and mediums as a way to drive their business. In effect, ciga-rette companies have been forced to develop a whole new set of skills."

Skills that include worldwide sports sponsorship—namely NASCAR and Formula One. NASCAR (the National Associ-ation for Stock Car Auto Racing) oversees approximately 1,500 races annually at over 100 tracks in America, Canada, and Mex-ico, and televises its races in over 150 countries. In the United States, it's the second-most popular professional sport in terms of TV ratings, ranking behind only the National Football League, and its approximately 75 million fans purchase over $3 billion in annual licensed product sales. According to the NASCAR Web site, NASCAR's fans "are considered the most brand-loyal in all of sports and as a result, Fortune 500 com-panies sponsor NASCAR more than any other governing body."[12]

Formula One has its roots and popularity throughout Europe, which remains its leading market, and hosts a series of highly publicized Grands Prix—a sport whose far-reaching popularity makes it another obvious sponsorship bonanza.

Why? Think about it: if your ads have been knocked off TV and banned by governments around the world, what better way to convey that feeling of risk, cool, youth, dynamism, raciness, and living on the edge (as opposed to, say, being tethered to a respirator) than to sponsor a car race? What about sponsoring the Ferrari team during its Formula One races? Paint a car Marlboro-red. Dress the driver and the crew in bright red jumpsuits. Then sit back in your box seat and exhale.

How effective are these underground tactics? It was time to put subliminal tobacco advertising to the test, using two iconic and enormously popular brands: Marlboro and Camel.

SEVERAL MONTHS BEFORE conducting the study I described in Chapter 1 about the efficacy—or, as it turned out, the lack thereof—of health warnings on cigarette packs, we'd shown our American volunteers one of the most repulsive (and to my mind, effective) antismoking TV ads I'd ever seen. A group of people are sitting around chatting and smoking. They're having a jolly good time, except for one problem: instead of smoke, thick, greenish-yellow globules of fat are pouring out of the tips of their cigarettes, congealing, coalescing, and splattering onto their ashtrays. The more the smokers talk and gesture, the more those caterpillar-sized wads of fat end up on the table, the floor, their shirtsleeves, all over the place. The point being, of course, that smoking spreads these same globules of fat throughout your blood-stream, clogging up your arteries and wreaking havoc with your health.

But just as with the cigarette warning labels, viewing this ad had caused our respondents' craving spots to come alive. They weren't put off by the gruesome images of artery-clogging fat; they barely even noticed them. Instead, their brains' mirror neurons latched on to the convivial atmosphere they were observing—and their "craving spots" were activated. Another powerful antismoking message had been taken down, just like that.

In other words, overt, direct, visually explicit antismoking messages did more to encourage smoking than any deliberate campaign Marlboro or Camel could have come up with. But now it was time to put *subliminal* tobacco ads to the test.

A good-looking cowboy with a rugged landscape stretched out behind him. Two men loping along on horseback. A hill-side in the American West. A jeep, speeding down a curving mountain road. A lipstick-colored sunset. A parched desert. Bright red Ferraris. Racing paraphernalia from both Formula 1 and NASCAR, including red cars and mechanics wearing signature red jumpsuits. These were among the images we showed our volunteers.

The images had two things in common. First, they were all associated with cigarette commercials from back in the era when governments permitted cigarette advertising (and don't forget that regardless of whether our smokers could actually remember these images from growing up, they're still ubiqui-tous online, in stores and cafés, and through viral marketing). Second, not a single cigarette, logo, or brand name was any-where in sight.

Over a two-month period, our smokers filed in and out of Dr. Calvert's laboratory. What parts of their brains would light up as they watched these logo-free images?

All of our subjects were asked to refrain from smoking for two hours preceding the test, to ensure that their nicotine levels would be equal at the start of the experiment. First, both groups were shown subliminal images that had no overt connection to cigarette brands—the aforementioned western-style scenery, including iconic cowboys, beautiful sunsets, and arid deserts. Next, to establish a comparison, they were shown explicit cigarette advertising images like the Marlboro Man and Joe Camel on his motorbike, as well as Marlboro and Camel logos. Dr. Calvert and I wanted to find out if the subliminal images would generate cravings similar to the ones generated by the logos and the clearly marked Marlboro and Camel packs.

To no one's surprise, the fMRI scans revealed a pronounced response in the volunteers' nucleus accumbens—the area we now know to be involved with reward, craving, and addiction—when they viewed the actual cigarette packs. But what was more interesting was that when the smokers were exposed to the nonexplicit images—the red Ferrari, the cowboys on horseback, the camel in a desert—over a period of less than five seconds, there was an almost immediate activity in the craving regions of their brains as well, in the exact same regions that responded to the explicit images of the packs and logos. In fact, the only consistent difference was that the subliminal images prompted more activity in the volunteers' primary visual cortex—as might be expected given the more complex visual task of processing those images.

More fascinating still, when Dr. Calvert compared the

brains' responses to the two different types of images, she found even *more* activity in the reward and craving centers when subjects viewed the subliminal images than when they viewed the overt images. In other words, the logo-free images *associated* with cigarettes, like the Ferrari and the sunset, triggered *more* cravings among smokers than the logos or the images of the cigarette packs themselves—a result that was consistent for both Camel and Marlboro smokers.

We also discovered a direct emotional relationship between the qualities the subjects associated with Formula 1 and NASCAR—masculinity, sex, power, speed, innovation, coolness—and the cigarette brands that sponsored them. In other words, when consumers were exposed to those red Ferraris and racer jumpsuits, they subconsciously linked those associations to the brand. In short, everything Formula 1 and NASCAR represent was subliminally transformed, in only seconds, into representing the *brand*.

In answer to the question, does subliminal advertising work, one would have to say yes—chillingly well. But why?

One reason is that since the subliminal images didn't show any visible logos, the smokers weren't consciously aware that they were viewing an advertising message, and as a result they let their guard down. Pretend that it's thirty years ago (back when cigarette ads were legal), and you're a smoker. You see an ad in a magazine or on a billboard. You know the ad is for cigarettes because the Camel logo is prominently positioned in the bottom corner. Immediately you raise your guard. You know that smoking is bad for your health, not to mention expensive, and that you'll be giving it up any day now. So you consciously construct a wall between yourself and the message, protecting yourself from its seductive powers. But once the logo vanishes, your brain is no longer on high alert, and it responds subconsciously—and enthusiastically—to the message before you.

Another explanation lies in the carefully manufactured associations that the tobacco industry has established over the past few decades. In 1997, in preparation for the ban on tobacco advertising that was about to come into place in the United Kingdom, Silk Cut, a popular British tobacco brand, began to position its logo against a background of purple silk in every ad that it ran. It didn't take long for consumers to associate this plain swath of purple silk with the Silk Cut logo, and eventually with the brand itself. So when the advertising ban came into effect, and the logo was no longer permitted on ads or billboards, the company simply created highway billboards that didn't say a word about Silk Cut or cigarettes but merely showcased logo-free swaths of purple silk. And guess what? Shortly after, a research study revealed that an astonishing 98 percent of consumers identified those billboards as having something to do with Silk Cut, although most were unable to say exactly why.

In other words, the tobacco companies' efforts to link "innocent images"—whether of the American West, purple silk, or sports cars—with smoking in our subconscious minds have paid off big time. They have succeeded in bypassing governments' regulations by creating stimuli powerful enough to replace traditional advertising. And in fact, they've even managed to enlist the help of governments all over the world; by banning tobacco advertising, governments are unwittingly *helping* to promote the deadly behavior they seek to eliminate.

For me, these results were a revelation. I speak at an enormous number of conferences every year, all around the globe. At each and every one, I'm exposed to literally hundreds of logos displayed on the walls, on brochures, on bags, on pens, and that's just for starters. For companies, the logo is regarded as king, the be-all and end-all of advertising. But as our study had just shown with what my research team assured me was 99 percent scientific certainty, the logo was, if not dead, then certainly on life support; that the thing we thought was most powerful in advertising was in fact the *least* so. Because, as our study had proved, far more potent than any cigarette logo were images associated with smoking, whether it was a red sports car or an aura of romantic solitude against a backdrop of the American Rockies.

So what are the *least* powerful ads in prompting you to smoke? Tobacco ads *without* warning disclaimers. Followed by ads *with* warning disclaimers—which make the ads all that more enticing—then merchandising (ashtrays, hats, you-name-it). More powerful still was the subliminal imagery, particularly the Formula 1/NASCAR race association. It's a little scary to find out that what we thought had the least to do with smoking is actually the most effective in making us want to smoke, and that the logo—what advertisers and companies have long endowed with almost mythic powers—in fact works the least well.

Can you imagine a world without logos? No headlines. No taglines. Can you imagine wordless ads that you could look at and know immediately what brand they were selling? Many companies, like Abercrombie & Fitch and Ralph Lauren, and as we've just seen, Philip Morris, have already begun to use logo-free advertising, and to great effect, too. In the future, many brands will follow suit. So remember, subliminal messages are out there. Don't let yourself—and your wallet—fall prey to them.

WHEN YOU GET dressed in the morning, do you always put your left shoe on first? When you go to the mall, do you always park in the same section of the parking lot, even though there are closer spots elsewhere? Do you have a lucky pen you always take to important meetings at work? Do you fearfully refuse to open an umbrella indoors? If so, you're not alone. In the next chapter, we're going to take a look at the extent to which rituals and superstitions govern our "rational" lives—and how most of the time, we don't even notice it.

5

**DO YOU BELIEVE
IN MAGIC?**

*Ritual, Superstition,
and Why We Buy*

LET'S PRETEND WE'RE AT a beachfront bar in Acapulco, enjoying the mellow ocean breeze. Two ice-cold Coronas coming right up, along with two slices of lime. We give the limes a squeeze, then stick them inside the necks of our bottles, tip the bottles upside down until the bubbles begin to get that nice fizz, and take a sip. Cheers.

But first, let me pester you with a multiple choice question. The Corona beer-and-lime ritual we just performed—any idea how that might have come about? A) Drinking beer with a lime wedge is simply the way Latino cultures quaff their Coronas, as it enhances the beer's taste. B) The ritual derives from an ancient Mesoamerican habit designed to combat germs, since the lime's acidity destroys any bacteria that may have formed on the bottle during packaging and shipping. C) The Corona-lime ritual reportedly dates back to 1981, when on a random bet with his buddy, a bartender at an unnamed restaurant popped a lime wedge into the neck of a Corona to see if he could get other patrons to do the same.

If you guessed C, you'd be right. And in fact, this simple, not-even-thirty-year-old ritual invented on a whim by a bartender during a slow night is generally credited with helping Corona overtake Heineken in the U.S. market.

Now let's switch scenes, to some dimly lit Irish joint with a name like Donnelly's or McClanahan's. Shamrocks everywhere, a counterful of old guys, a bartender who's heard every story twice. We take seats at the bar and order. Two Guinnesses, please. First the bartender pours the glass three-quarters full. Then we wait (and wait) until the foamy head settles. Finally, once just the right amount of time has elapsed, the bartender tops it off. This all takes a couple of minutes, but neither of us minds the wait—fact is, the ritual of the slow pour is part of the pleasure of drinking a Guinness in the first place. But here's what I'll bet you didn't know: this ritual didn't come about by accident. In the time-choked culture of the early 1990s, Guinness was facing big losses in pubs across the British Isles. Why? Customers didn't want to wait ten minutes for the head of their beer to settle. So the company decided to turn this annoyance into a virtue. They rolled out advertising campaigns like, "Good things come to those who wait," and "It takes 119.53 seconds to pour the perfect pint," and even aired commercials showing the "right" way to pour a Guinness. Soon, a ritual was born. And thanks to the company's clever advertising, the artful pour became part of the drinking experience. "We just don't want *anyone* putting liquid in a glass," Guinness brewmeister Fergal Murray was once quoted as saying.[1]

In all my years helping companies develop and strengthen their brands, there's one thing I've seen time and time again: rituals help us form emotional connections with brands and products. They make the things we buy memorable. But before I explain why, it's worth taking a look at the extent to which ritual and superstition govern our lives.

RITUALS AND SUPERSTITIONS are defined as not entirely rational actions and the belief that one can somehow manipulate the future by engaging in certain behaviors, in spite of the fact there's no discernible causal relationship between that behavior and its outcome.

But if such beliefs are so irrational, why do most of us act in superstitious ways every day, without even thinking about it?

As we all know, it's a stressful world out there. Natural disasters. Wars. Hunger. Torture. Global warming. These are just a few of the issues that bombard us every time we turn on the TV, crack open a newspaper, or go onto the Web. Let's face it: our world is changing at an astonishingly rapid rate. Technology is advancing at speeds we never could have imagined, seismic shifts in global economic power are happening overnight—hell, we're even *walking* faster than we used to (a 2007 analysis of pedestrians in thirty-four cities around the world showed that the average pedestrian clips along at almost 3.5 mph—roughly 10 percent faster than they did a decade ago). In my native Denmark, men and women even *talk* 20 percent faster than they did ten years ago.[2]

Such rapid change has brought with it more uncertainty. The more unpredictable the world becomes, the more we grope for a sense of control over our lives. And the more anxiety and uncertainty we feel, the more we adopt superstitious behavior and rituals to help shepherd us through. "The sense of having special powers buoys people in threatening situations, and helps soothe everyday fears and ward off mental distress," writes *New York Times* reporter Benedict Carey.[3]

Superstition and ritual have been scientifically linked to humans' need for control in a turbulent world. As Dr. Bruce Hood, professor of experimental psychology at the University of Bristol, in England, writes, "If you remove the appearance that they are in control, both humans and animals become stressed. During the Gulf War in 1991, in the areas that were attacked by Scud missiles, there was a rise in superstitious belief."

Indeed, when Giora Keinan, a professor at Tel Aviv University, sent questionnaires to 174 Israelis following the Iraqi Scud missile attacks of 1991, he found that those soldiers who reported the greatest level of stress were also the ones most likely to endorse magical beliefs. "I have the feeling that the chances of being hit during a missile attack are greater if a person whose house was attacked is present in the sealed room," one soldier reported, while another believed he was less likely to be hit if he had "stepped into the sealed room right foot first."[4] Rationally, of course, none of this makes the slightest bit of sense. But as Hood explains, even the most rational, analytically minded of us can fall prey to this kind of thinking.

Hood went on to prove his point during an address at the British Association Festival of Science in Norwich. In front of a roomful of scientists, Hood held up a blue sweater and offered ten pounds to anyone who agreed to try it on. Hands flew up all over the room. Hood then told the audience that the sweater once belonged to Fred West, a serial killer who was believed to have brutally murdered twelve young women, as well as his own wife. All but a handful of those same hands shot down.[5] And when the few remaining volunteers *did* try on the sweater, Hood observed that their fellow audience members edged away from them. Hood then confessed that the piece of clothing *didn't* actually belong to Fred West, but that was irrelevant. The mere *suggestion* that the sweater had been worn by the killer was enough to make the scientists shy away. It was "as if evil, a moral stance defined by culture, has become physically manifest inside the clothing," said Hood. Rationally or not, we unwittingly ascribe similar power to objects such as "lucky" coins, wedding rings, and so on.

But are superstitions and rituals necessarily bad for us? Interestingly, some rituals have actually been shown to be beneficial to our mental and physical well-being. According to a study published in the *Journal of Family Psychology,* "In families with predictable routines, children had fewer respiratory illnesses and better overall health, and they performed better in elementary school." The article added that rituals have a greater effect on emotional health, and that in families with strong rituals adolescents "reported a stronger sense of self, couples reported happier marriages and children had greater interaction with their grandparents."[6]

A 2007 study carried out by global advertising giant BBDO Worldwide showed that across twenty-six countries around the world, most of us perform a common, predictable series of rituals from the moment we get up in the morning to the moment we pull down our covers at night. The first is one the company labels "preparing for battle," when we rise up from our cocoons of sleep and prepare to face the day. Preparing for battle can include everything from brushing our teeth, to taking a bath or shower, to checking our e-mail, to shaving, to scanning the headlines of the morning paper—whatever helps us feel a sense of control over whatever the upcoming day may bring.

A second ritual is what's known as "feasting," which involves eating meals with others. It might be a sushi dinner with a group of friends at a familiar restaurant, or a family eating breakfast together. Whatever our exact ritual, the social act of eating together is important; it "reunites us with our tribe," transforming us from solitary beings to members of a group.

"Sexing up" is third on the list. It's self-explanatory—a pleasant and indulgent series of rituals that transform us from our workaday selves to our best-looking, most confident beings. Our sexing up rituals involve all manners of primping and grooming, as well as asking friends for reassurance and validation—*How do I look? Is this outfit all right?*—and chatting about the upcoming evening.

A final daily ritual is called "protecting yourself from the future." This involves all acts we perform before going to bed at night—turning off computers and lights, lowering the heat, setting the burglar alarm, checking on children and pets, locking the doors and windows, and parking packed bags and briefcases by the door so we won't forget them in the morning. As the final ritual of the day, protecting yourself from the future helps us feel secure before the next day arrives and we start a new round of rituals all over again.[7]

These rituals have everything to do with gaining control— or at least the illusion of it—and we all perform them in one shape or form every day. But many of us also carry out other, less productive rituals that are grounded in superstition or irrational beliefs—and most of us aren't even aware of it. Just for fun, let's walk through an imaginary week.

You awaken early Monday morning to overcast skies and heavy rain (as usual, you've set your alarm clock ahead ten minutes). Upon arriving at work, you go out of your way to avoid walking under a workman's ladder in the lobby. At lunch, you make your way to the outdoor fountain in a nearby park. You fumble around in your pants or purse for a coin, briefly make a wish—please, let me get that promotion—then toss the coin in. You walk back to the office feeling a little silly, yet more at ease.

The sun returns on Tuesday, and you decide you'll walk to work. Traipsing down a crowded sidewalk, you recall the distant memory of a childhood rhyme: *Step on a crack, break your mother's back.* That afternoon, the wish you made at the fountain comes true—you got the promotion you wanted. You know you won it because of your hard work, but you can't help but give some credit to the coin you cast into the fountain.

On Wednesday, you greet a friend at a Chinese restaurant, kissing her on both cheeks—a European ritual you adopted after vacationing in France. After your meal, you crack open your fortune cookie to read your fortune. Your dining companion sneezes, and you murmur *Gesundheit,* roughly "bless you" in German and Yiddish. As you're leaving the table you slip your fortune-cookie fortune into your wallet. You'll be playing those numbers the next time you buy a lottery ticket. (On March 30, 2007, 110 people played the same numbers they found on the back of a fortune cookie—22, 28, 32, 33,

39, 40—and became second-prize Powerball winners, taking home anywhere from $100,000 to $500,000, costing the lottery association nearly $19 million.[8])

Friday, as it happens, falls on the thirteenth of the month. Noting the date, you feel a surge of anxiety. You take a quick glance at your horoscope—nothing bad there. With Christmas approaching, you buy a tree, decorate it with lights, ornaments, and tinsel—saving the star for last—and finally tape mistletoe over all your doorways, not that you really believe anyone will angle you under a sprig for a kiss.

On Saturday, you go to a wedding. It's raining—bad luck for the bride and groom (or is it good luck? It's one or the other). At the reception, you join the throng in tossing rice at the newlyweds, and drink a champagne toast to their health and marriage. Do you really believe that knocking back a glass of Kava will ensure them a lifetime of good health and wedded bliss? Of course not. But the point is, most rituals and superstitious behaviors are so ingrained in our culture and daily lives that we often don't even think about why we're doing them.

Nor is such behavior limited exclusively to American culture. Take the fear of the number thirteen, for example. In early 2007, in response to countless customer complaints, Brussels Airlines reluctantly altered the thirteen dots in their airline logo to fourteen.[9] If you want to sit in the thirteenth row on your Air France, KLM, Iberia (or for that matter, Continental) flight, you're plain out of luck, as there isn't one. Last year, on one Friday the thirteenth, the number of car accidents shot up by 51 percent in London and 32 percent in Germany—most likely due to drivers' heightened anxiety about the unlucky date. Other numbers, too, have been associated with bad luck. After two Flight 191s crashed, Delta and American each permanently retired the flight number.[10]

In Asian cultures, the unluckiest possible number is four, since the Mandarin word for that number is read as *si,* which comes perilously close in sound to *shi,* which means "death." As a result, in hotels in China, and even in Asian-owned hotels around the world, there are no fourth or forty-fourth floors. California researcher David Phillips even found that heart attacks among U.S. residents of Chinese descent spiked as much as 13 percent on the fourth day of every month. In California, where there is a strong influence of Chinese culture, the ratio was even higher, reaching a peak of 27 percent. Like the Friday the thirteenth car crashes in Germany and London, the spike was probably due, in Phillips's opinion, to the sheer stress inspired by the cultural fear of four.[11]

On the other hand, eight is a lucky number in Asian cultures, as it sounds similar to the Chinese word signifying "wealth," "fortune," and "prosper." This explains why the Summer Olympics in Beijing was slated to get officially under way on 8/08/08 at exactly 8:08:08 p.m. And listen to this: during a license plate auction held in the capital city of Guangzhou, one Chinese man bid 54,000 yuan—that's $6,750, or approximately seven times China's per capita income—on a license plate simply because it read APY*888.* This record was later smashed by a man who bid 80,000 yuan, or $10,568, on a license plate that had only two eights: AC66*88.* Chinese cell phone carriers charge premiums for "lucky" phone numbers, and one regional Chinese airline is said to have paid roughly $2.4 million yuan—that's US$300,000—for an 888-8888 exchange.[12]

Eights aren't the only good-luck talismans in Japan, either. Kit Kats, the classic candy bar, are considered lucky, too. When Nestlé rolled out their candy in the Far East, locals couldn't help but notice how close the words "Kit Kat" were to "Kitto-Katsu," which roughly translates to "win without fail." In time, students began to believe that eating a Kit Kat before they took their exams would result in a higher grade, which is a major reason the Kit Kat brand is doing so well in Japan's overcrowded retail market. Nestlé went one step further by rolling out their Kit Kats in a blue bag—to make people think of the sky, as in Heaven—and printing the words "Prayers to God" on the package. It seems that Kit Kats are scoring in Asia not just because they are considered good luck, but because on the Nestlé Web site, browsers can enter a prayer that they believe will be sent up to a higher power.

Superstitions and rituals, of course, are a big part of the sporting world, too. Patrick Roy, the NHL goaltender, made it a rule to avoid skating on the rink's blue lines, and had a ritual of engaging his goalposts in a nightly heart-to-heart chat. Michael Jordan never played a game without his old Carolina Tar Heels shorts tucked underneath his yellow Chicago Bulls uniform, and former baseball star Wade Boggs refused to eat anything but chicken on game days. He also stepped to the plate for batting practice at exactly 5:17 p.m. each day, and traced the Hebrew sign for *chai*, which means "life," on the dirt before each time at bat (he's not Jewish, either).

Athletes believe in the supernatural powers of "hot" streaks, too—those times when they just can't seem to miss a single pitch, shot, goal, or basket. When a player shoots a string of good shots in a game, it's generally believed he has the "hot hand." The team then conspires to get him the ball because they believe he's on some kind of roll. In 1985, two future Nobel Prize–winning economists, Daniel Kahneman and Amos Tversky, unsettled basketball fans across the United States when they disproved this myth, well known to both players and fans.

To test whether or not these "hot streaks" actually exist, Kahneman and Tversky examined the statistics for a number of teams from 1980 to 1982. When they analyzed the Boston Celtics' free-throw ratio, they discovered that if a player made his first shot, he made the second shot 75 percent of the time. But when the player missed the first shot, the likelihood of making the second shot remained exactly the same. And when they scrutinized the scoring streaks and free-throw records of individual players at home games, Kahneman and Tversky concluded that none of the players were statistically any more likely to make a second shot when it followed a first good shot. The "hot hand," it turns out, is decidedly more a matter of faith—and superstition—than of fact.

Or what about the ritual of the Olympic flame, which runners transport around the world in the globe's largest relay race (though, in fact, the Olympic flame is a ritual that began not thousands of years ago in Ancient Greece, as many people believe, but at the 1936 Berlin Olympics)? If you think about it, the Olympic Games would be next to nothing if you took away its rituals. Imagine, no opening and closing ceremonies, no presentation of the winners' medals after each contest, no stirring national anthems. What in the world would be left? In fact, most of what we enjoy in the world of sports and entertainment today wouldn't be the same without the rituals.

*   *   *

BUT WHAT DO rituals have to do with what we think about
when we buy? A lot. For one thing, products and brands that
have rituals or superstitions associated with them are much
"stickier" than those that don't. In an unsettled, fast-moving
world, we're all searching for stability and familiarity, and
product rituals give us an illusion of comfort and belonging.
Isn't there a sense of security in being part of, say, the Apple
community or the Netflix community—in knowing that there
are millions of other people out there who listen to their iPods
every morning on the train or who cue up a new list of movies
every Friday night, just like you do?

In an increasingly standardized, sterilized, homogenous
world (how many malls have you visited with the exact same
stores—a Staples, a Gap, a Best Buy, a Chili's, and a Banana
Republic? Too many, I'll bet), rituals help us differentiate one
brand from another. And once we find a ritual or brand we
like, isn't there a lot of comfort in having a particular blend of
coffee to brew every morning, a signature shampoo with a familiar smell, or a favorite make of running sneaker we buy
year after year? I'd even venture to say that there is something
so appealing about this sense of stability and familiarity that a
lot of consumers have almost a religious sense of loyalty to
their favorite brands and products.

Indeed, buying a product is more often a ritualized behavior than a conscious decision. Take skin creams. Do those
antiwrinkle, smile-line-eliminating, crows'-feet-exiling potions
that beckon to every woman (and more and more men) from

the drugstore shelves actually work? Many female consumers I've observed over the years admit that antiwrinkle creams are pointless, but every three months, they'll still clamber to the local pharmacy to pick up the latest miracle balm, the one with the newest, sexiest, most complex-sounding secret formula. It's a pattern as predictable as the seasons. After a few weeks, they'll gaze disappointedly into their mirrors, conclude it doesn't work, and go out to hunt down another magic formula. Why? Simply because it's a ritual they—and their mothers and grandmothers before them—have always followed.

After all, most of us are creatures of habit. Consider the way we navigate a cell phone. Once we become accustomed to Nokia's navigational keys, aren't we loath to change brands to, say, a Sony Ericsson? Who wants to relearn an entirely new system? Consumers who own an Apple iPod are no doubt accustomed to its ritualized navigation; most iPod users could press Music, then Artists, followed by their favorite track in their sleep. Why court confusion by buying an mp3 player made by Phillips or a Microsoft Zune? Whether you know it or not, you don't want to tamper with the region of your brain made up of your "implicit" memory, which encompasses everything you know how to do without thinking about it, from riding a bike to parallel-parking to tying your shoelaces to buying a book effortlessly on Amazon.

Food rituals, too, can be found everywhere: from how we always break the wishbone after a Thanksgiving dinner to how we like to eat our Oreo cookie. When it comes to Oreos, there are two distinct rituals. Some people like to pry open the cookie, lick off the white frosting in between, then eat the two wafers. Others like to keep the sandwich cookie intact, and dunk the whole thing in a glass of cold milk. Knowing how many people enjoy the ritual of eating Oreos with milk, Nabisco, which manufactures Oreos, recently partnered up with the producers of the popular "Got Milk?" campaign. "Oreo is not just a cookie, it's a ritual," confirms Mike Faherty, senior category business director for Oreo. "Dunking Oreo cookies in milk is part of the American fabric."[13]

An Irish brand of cider known as Magners has recently exploded in popularity in the United Kingdom. Why? The company didn't tweak its recipe. It didn't hire a celebrity spokesperson. It didn't roll out some wacky new line extension, say, a Magners candy bar. So what's the secret to its sudden success? Years ago, the majority of pubs in the Irish county of Tipperary lacked fridges, so consumers took it upon themselves to cool down Magners by pouring it over ice. From then on, bartenders served Magners from a large bottle into a pint glass, using lots of ice. Turns out that making the cider colder cut its sweetness and improved its taste. From then on, bartenders served Magners from a large bottle into a pint glass, using lots of ice, and a ritual was born. This not only improved the taste of the cider, but also went so far as to redefine what consumers thought of when they thought about the brand. In time, the ritual became so linked to the cider that people began to refer to the brand as "Magners on Ice."[14]

Other edible brands have made rituals out of their sheer seasonal availability. Take Mallomars, a chocolate biscuit coated in a layer of dark chocolate that tends to melt in hot weather. To avoid Mallomar-meltdown, Nabisco halts production every year from April to September. But as soon as the weather begins to cool down, Mallomar addicts begin awaiting Mallomars' reappearance on supermarket shelves the way some nature lovers await the swallows of Capistrano. "News of the wonders of refrigerator and climate control has apparently not reached Nabisco's New Jersey headquarters," one article concludes dryly, suggesting that the company has artificially manufactured this ritual by limiting the cookies availability.[15] And as with Oreos, there are several sanctioned methods to eat a Mallomar—by biting off the marshmallow part and saving the graham cracker for last, reversing the entire process, or eating the thing whole.

Even some restaurants have rituals you probably haven't even considered. At Subway sandwich franchises, sandwiches are constructed in the same order each time, so customers know precisely how to instruct the person behind the counter to make their sandwich. Cold Stone Creamery, the popular ice cream chain, has an interesting ritual—its servers treat customers to a song and dance along with their ice cream. And speaking of food rituals, do you eat your Big Mac with two hands instead of one? Do you eat your French fries before your burger, or after, or in alternating bites? (and didn't their smell inspire you to order them in the first place?) And, like me, do you not even think about these rituals when you're doing them?

Sometimes, however, brands can have trouble moving beyond rituals. Take the ritual of drinking Bacardi with Coke with a slice of lime (otherwise known as a Cuba Libre), a combination that came about in 1898 during the Spanish-American War, when American soldiers were stationed in Cuba. The country was then the headquarters for Bacardi and when the U.S. forces brought in their Cokes, a lasting union of two flavors was created. But today, Bacardi finds itself a little bit trapped. They'd like customers to feel free to mix their rums with other mixers, but the rum-and-Coke ritual has proven a pretty powerful one to shake.

BUT SUPERSTITIONS AND rituals can take forms that go beyond how we eat an Oreo or pour a cocktail. There are many other ways we often can behave irrationally when it comes to products. When I was around five years old, I contracted an extremely bizarre disease known as Schonlein-Henochs, an allergic reaction that typically follows a respiratory tract infection, symptoms of which include internal bleeding and kidney inflammation. I turned as red as a Christmas stocking.

For more than a month, I was confined to a hospital bed in a sound-isolated room. It was painful to move. I couldn't bear even the slightest noise, as it hurt my ears. I was extremely sick for two years. When the disease finally went away, my doctors still wouldn't let me play any contact sports. So I would have something to do while everybody else my age was outside playing football, my parents gave me a box of Legos.

Bad move. It was the beginning of a decade-long love affair.

I'm persistent and obsessive by nature, and from that day on, I began collecting boxful after boxful of Legos. They became my life. I stowed my collection in a drawer under the lower mattress of my bunk bed, though usually hundreds of Legos were strewn all over my bedroom floor. A year later, I entered my first big construction—a replica of a Scandinavian ferryboat—in a local Lego competition. Once the Lego jury proved that I'd built the thing without any help from my parents (they rather sadistically destroyed the boat and made me rebuild it), I was awarded first prize.

Which was—guess what—another big box of Legos. Energized by my success, I came up with the idea of constructing my own version of Legoland. Colonizing my parents' backyard, I built canals, bridges, a boat, a castle, and even a complicated sensor system. I traveled to Sweden to get a special kind of grainy rock and a special brand of foam for my mountains. I bought my own custom-made engine to power the canal system—there was even a mini-landscape of bonsai trees. (I was eleven at the time—what can I say?)

Finally, I opened up my Legoland in my parents' backyard, with pathways around it for spectators. When no one showed up, I was heartbroken. So I placed an ad in the local paper, and this time 131 people came—including two lawyers from Lego, who informed me very politely that if I persisted in using the name Legoland, I'd be guilty of trademark infringement. In the end, after lots of back and forth, I ended up renaming my version Mini-Land. (A few years later, I found myself working for the Lego company, but that's another story.)

The point is I know a little something about collecting, and a lot about obsession with a brand. And in many ways, brand obsession has a lot in common with rituals and superstitious behavior—both involve habitual, repeated actions that have little or no logical basis, and both stem from the need for a sense of control in an overwhelming and complex world.

As a society bred from hunters and gatherers, we're all hardwired to accumulate, though these days, collecting has reached extreme levels. A 1981 *New York Times* article, "Living with Collections," estimated that approximately 30 percent of

Americans tend to hoard—and their number is growing, thanks largely to the secondary markets that the Internet has created. In 1995, the same year eBay opened up their site, sales in the collectibles industry reached $8.2 billion. Currently there are 49 million users—many of them collectors—registered on the eBay Web site.

In ancient times, collecting was the exclusive province of the rich, but nowadays, people of all income levels accumulate everything from Barbie dolls and Happy Meal toys to Coke bottles and Campbell's Soup cans, to sneakers and Fillmore West posters. To take an extreme example, today more than twenty-two thousand different Hello Kitty products are in circulation in Asia and throughout the world, including Hello Kitty pasta, Hello Kitty condoms, Hello Kitty navel rings, and Hello Kitty tooth caps, which (talk about branding) actually leave behind a Hello Kitty impression on every piece of food you chew. On Eva Air, Taipei's second largest airline, armed with a Hello Kitty boarding pass, you make your way to your seat to await the arrival of stewardesses dressed in Hello Kitty aprons and Hello Kitty hair ribbons serving snacks in Hello Kitty shapes—and even selling Hello Kitty duty-free items.

Less extreme cases of brand obsession typically take root in adolescence and even earlier. If children experience social difficulties in school, studies have shown they're far more likely to become preoccupied with collecting. Collecting something—whether it's coins, stamps, leaves, Pokémon cards, or Beanie Babies—gives children a sense of mastery, completion, and control, while at the same time raising their self-esteem, elevating their status, and just maybe even compensating for earlier years of social difficulty.

Point is, there's something about the ritual-like act of collecting that makes us feel safe and secure. When we are stressed out, or when life feels random and out-of-control, we often seek out comfort in familiar products or objects. We want to have solid, consistent patterns in our lives, and in our brands. So, even though our rational brains tell us it's completely irrational and illogical to own 547 Hello Kitty fridge magnets, we buy them anyway, because the collecting ritual makes us feel somehow more in control of our lives.[16]

ONE THING IS clear. Ritual and superstition can exert a potent influence on how and what we buy. And after years of studying product rituals and their effect on branding, it struck me: might religion—which is so steeped in familiar and comforting rituals of its own—play a role in why we buy as well?

In my next experiment, I set out to discover what connection, if any, exists between religion and our buying behavior. Are there similarities between the way our brains react to religious and spiritual symbols, and the way they react to products or brands? Would certain brands provoke the same kind of emotions in us or inspire the same sense of devotion and loyalty provoked by religion? I wasn't trying to downplay the importance of religion in people's lives, but I was pretty sure there was something here.

Turns out I was right.

6

I SAY A LITTLE
PRAYER

Faith, Religion, and Brands

ONE BY ONE, OVER THE
course of several days, the nuns filed into the laboratory,
smoothed out their black and white habits, and made themselves as comfortable as possible on the fMRI's examination
table. Ranging in age from twenty-three to sixty-four, the fifteen women participating in this 2006 study were members of
the cloistered Carmelite order, an austere Roman Catholic sect
of monastics whose roots go back to medieval times.

Overseen by Dr. Mario Beauregard and Dr. Vincent
Paquette, two neuroscientists at the University of Montreal,
Canada, the "nun study" wasn't carried out to further any religious agenda or to prove or disprove the existence of God.
It was simply to use neuroimaging to find out more about how
the brain experiences religious feelings or beliefs. Beauregard
and Paquette were attempting to uncover the answer to a
complex question: what parts of our brains light up when
we're engaging in private, spiritual experiences, such as prayer,

or when we're experiencing the sensation that we're close to God?

The scientists began by asking the fifteen nuns to relive the most profound religious experience they'd had as members of the Carmelite order.[1] Unsurprisingly, the scans revealed that when reliving those experiences, the nuns exhibited a flurry of neural activity in their caudate nucleus, a small, central brain region that produces feelings of joy, serenity, self-awareness, and even love. Another activated area was the insula, which the scientists theorized relates to feelings associated with connections to the divine.

Then, the scientists asked the nuns to relive a profound emotional experience they'd had with another human being. Interestingly, the activity recorded in these scans was markedly different.

In short, Beauregard and Paquette concluded that while there is no single "God Spot" in the human brain, no one discrete region that's activated when we're engaged in religious or spiritual thoughts, there are—at least among those with strong religious beliefs—different patterns of activity when thinking about religion and when thinking about other human beings. As the next part of our study would show, when it comes to religion and faith, a number of integrated, interconnected brain regions work simultaneously and in tandem. Or, as a quote I once stumbled across said, "Trying to draw strict borders around consciousness is like trying to stick Post-it notes on the ocean."

*   *   *

THIS STUDY WAS part of my inspiration for my next brain-scan research experiment. But it wasn't as if my theory about brands and spirituality had come out of nowhere. Consider the following story:

One early winter afternoon in 2007, a small, excited crowd gathered at the storage bin at Port Newark in New Jersey, awaiting the arrival of a simple container. Most of the on-lookers were formally dressed in white gloves, long black coats, and wide-brimmed hats. A rabbi stood in the center of the group, while a few photographers snapped away. At last, the hatch of the ship's hold opened, and from the darkness a fastidiously dressed man emerged carrying a silver tray containing packages of . . . dirt.

But this wasn't ordinary dirt. This was holy dirt, brought to our shores courtesy of Holy Land Earth, a Brooklyn-based company, the first business in the world to export soil directly from Israel to the United States. But what do people want with Israeli dirt, you might be wondering? Well, as it turns out, a handful of soil from the Holy Land can add a perfect touch of the sacred to religious burials. It can also be used to bless plants and trees, houses and buildings.

Among the assembled throng was Holy Land Earth's founder and president, Steven Friedman, who addressed the dockside crowd. Many religions consider the ground of Israel to be sacred, he explained; his company was now importing this divine soil to anyone who wanted a small piece of the Holy Land in their lives. In fact, the soil had the official stamp of approval from Rabbi Velvel Brevda, the director of the Council of Geula in Jerusalem. "This is the culmination of many years of hard work," Friedman proclaimed. "It took quite a bit of effort to not only satisfy import regulations, but to make sure our product had the endorsement of recognized Jewish religious leaders." But it was all worth it, Friedman concluded.

Steven Friedman was hardly the first person to dabble in sacred dirt. In the late 1990s, an Irish immigrant named Alan Jenkins spent nine years securing U.S. government approval to import soil from Ireland. His reasoning? When the Irish came to America, they brought with them their churches, schools, and music—the only thing they had to leave behind was their soil. So, teaming up with an agricultural scientist, he doggedly petitioned both the U.S. Customs Department and the Animal and Plant Health Inspection Service to make Irish soil legally exportable, and eventually won.

To date Alan Jenkins has shipped more than $3 million worth of Irish soil—sold in 12-ounce plastic bags labeled Official Irish Dirt—to the United States. For Irish immigrants, the soil of their native land has an almost religious significance because, like many Jews, quite a few Irish immigrants pine to be buried in the soil of their homeland. An eighty-seven-year-old lawyer in Manhattan, originally from Galway, recently bought $100,000 worth of Irish dirt to fill up his American grave. Another Irishman hailing from County Cork spent $148,000 on a few tons to spread under the New England house he was building. Funeral directors and florists have ordered the topsoil by the ton. Even wholesalers in China have found dirt to be a lucrative business, as Chinese customers have been seduced by the legend of Irish luck.

If companies can make money off holy dirt, why not holy water? According to *Newsweek,* every bottle of "Holy Drinking Water, produced by a California-based company called

Wayne Enterprises, is blessed in the warehouse by an Anglican or Roman Catholic priest. Like a crucifix or a rosary, a bottle of Holy Drinking Water is a daily reminder to be kind to others," says Brian Germann, Wayne's CEO. Not to be outdone, a Florida company has just rolled out a product called Spiritual Water, which is basically purified municipal water, adorned with nearly a dozen different Christian labels. The Virgin Mary bottle, for example, has the Hail Mary prayer printed on the back in English and Spanish. According to founder Elicko Taieb, Spiritual Water helps people to "stay focused, believe in yourself and believe in God."[2]

If people are willing to pay sums large and small for things—like dirt and water—that they believe have religious or spiritual significance, then clearly spirituality and branding are inextricably linked. So I set out to prove it. But before I could attempt to identify the link between the two, I had to find out exactly what qualities characterize a religion in the first place. So in preparation for what would turn out to be one of the most provocative pieces of research I've conducted yet, I interviewed fourteen prominent leaders from various religions around the world—including Catholicism, Protestantism, Buddhism, and Islam—to find out what characteristics and qualities each of their faiths shared. What I discovered was that despite their differences, almost every leading religion has ten common pillars underlying its foundation: a sense of belonging, a clear vision, power over enemies, sensory appeal, storytelling, grandeur, evangelism, symbols, mystery, and rituals.

And just as I suspected, these pillars happen to have a great deal in common with our most beloved brands and products. Let's look at how.

Have you ever smiled knowingly at the person on the treadmill next to you when you notice he or she is wearing the same brand of running sneakers? Or honked and waved at the guy in the next lane because he's driving a Toyota Scion and so are you? My point is, whether you're in love with Nike, Neutrogena, Absolut, or Harley-Davidson, chances are you feel a sense of belonging among other users of that brand—it's like being a member of a not-so-exclusive club.

This sense of belonging is a profound influence on our behavior. Think about such seemingly unrelated groups as Weight Watchers at a meeting, the fans at the Super Bowl, and the audience at a Rolling Stones concert. These events bring together a group of people who share a similar mission, whether it's to conquer fat, win a trophy, or share in the collective joy of a musical extravaganza. In fact, Whittier College professor Joseph Price, who studies parallels between the worlds of sports and religion, has likened the Super Bowl to a religious pilgrimage. "A religious pilgrimage is more than just a journey to a place," he says. "It involves interior exploration, quests for a transcendent goal, overcoming barriers and physical or spiritual healing."[3]

Go Steelers.

Most religions also have a clear vision. By that I mean that they are unambiguous in their mission, whether it's to reach a certain state of grace or achieve a spiritual goal. And of course, most companies have unambiguous missions as well. Steve Jobs's vision for Apple dates back to the mid-1980s when he said, "Man is the creator of change in this world. As such he should be above systems and structures, and not subordinate to them." Twenty years and a few million iPods later, the company still pursues this vision, and will doubtlessly continue to do so twenty years from now. Or think about high-end audio and video product maker Bang & Olufsen's mission statement, "Courage to constantly question the ordinary in search of surprising, long-lasting experiences," or IBM's mandate, "Solutions for a Small Planet." Like religions, successful companies and successful brands have a clear, and very powerful, sense of mission.

Successful religions also strive to exert power over their enemies. Religious conflicts have existed since the beginning of time, and it doesn't take more than a glance at the news to see that taking sides against the Other is a potent uniting force. Having an identifiable enemy gives us the chance not only to articulate and showcase our faith, but also to unite ourselves with our fellow believers.

This kind of us vs. them mentality can be seen throughout the consumer world, as well. Coke vs. Pepsi, AT&T vs. Verizon, Visa vs. MasterCard. Think about the recent Hertz campaign, and its tagline "We're Hertz and they're not." Or the TV spots in which the Apple user, played by the cool, good-looking urban professional most guys aspire to be, and the PC user, the chubby, bespectacled geek, debate the respective merits of their operating systems (with the Apple user, of course, coming out on top). In fact, what commercial or ad campaign *doesn't* emphasize the reasons a given product is better than its competitors? This us-vs.-them strategy attracts fans, incites controversy, creates loyalty, and gets us thinking and arguing—and, of course, buying.

Sensory appeal (I'll explore this further in Chapter 8) is another key characteristic of the world's great religions. Close your eyes and walk into a church, a temple, or a mosque. You're immediately enveloped in the ambience of the building, as you smell the air, the incense, and the fragrance of the wood. If you open your eyes, you'll see the light reflect off the stained glass. Maybe a bell is sounding, or an organ is playing, or a priest or rabbi or minister is speaking. In a way, our senses allow us to "feel" the heart, soul, and sheer heft of a religion. Isn't the same true for products? Products and brands evoke certain feelings and associations based on how they look, feel, or smell. Think of the unmistakable sound of a Nokia ring tone. Or the pristine, leathery scent of a brand new Mercedes-Benz. Or the sleek, aesthetically pleasing lines of an iPod. Whether it's annoyance or longing, products' sensory qualities almost always evoke an emotional response. That's why, in 1996, Harley-Davidson took Yamaha and Honda to court for infringing on the copyright of the signature fast "potato-potato-potato" sound you hear when you rev up a Harley.

Or consider Toblerone. Chocolate in triangular shapes— now what's that all about? If Toblerone were rolling out its brand today, Wal-Mart probably wouldn't agree to carry it; the package isn't stackable. But it's the chocolate's appeal to our senses—its irregular shape, distinctively sweet taste, and hard, subtly bumpy texture—that makes it uniquely Toblerone, and that, in fact, is the secret of its success.

Another integral part of religion is storytelling. Whether the New Testament, the Torah, or the Koran, every religion is built upon a heft of history and stories—hundreds and hundreds of them (sometimes gruesome, sometimes miraculous, and oftentimes both). And the rituals that most religions draw upon and ask us to participate in—praying, kneeling, meditating, fasting, singing hymns, or receiving the Sacrament—are rooted in these stories upon which the faith is built.

In the same way, every successful brand has stories connected to it. Think of Disney, and all the colorful characters that instantly come to mind, from Mickey Mouse to Tinkerbell to Captain Jack Sparrow. Think of the small canisters of salt and pepper that you picked up the last time you flew to London on Virgin Atlantic, the ones that say *Nicked from Virgin Atlantic*. Or consider Whole Foods' recent decision to sell a limited number of bags inscribed with the oversized words *I'm Not a Plastic Bag*. If they're not plastic bags, what are they? It didn't matter. Sensing a story they could complete with their own meaning, consumers lined up in droves and the bags sold out almost immediately.

Most religions celebrate a sense of grandeur, as well (although a few emphasize austerity). Have you ever paid a visit to the Vatican? Among the vaulted ceilings and beautiful frescoes, the rich tapestries, furniture and paintings, one comes away with the realization that all of us are mere mortals, dwarfed by something far greater than ourselves. Preserving this sense of grandeur is so important, in fact, that no building in Rome is permitted to be higher than St. Peter's Cathedral. Think of the splendor of the Temple of the Golden Buddha in Bangkok, adorned with a nearly eleven-foot-tall Buddha. Made from solid gold, it weighs over two-and-a-half tons and is valued at nearly $200 million. Many companies similarly work to inspire feelings of awe and wonderment, from the Bellagio hotel in Las Vegas to Dubai's extraordinary (and extraordinarily weird-looking) Hotel Burj Al Arab, which seems to sit angled in the waters like a spaceship that's just toppled to earth. In fact, just think of any number of luxury brands—the Louis Vuitton flagship store in Paris, Prada's flagship store in Tokyo, Apple's flagship stores in New York and Chicago. All marketed to stir up notions of grandeur.

Certain companies and products inspire wonder just by the scope of their vision. Consider how Google Maps, with its ability to scan the landscape from Maine to Mars, has lent the company an omnipotent, omnipresent grandeur, as if they now own the maps of the skies and even outer space. And thanks to the vision of larger-than-life CEO Richard Branson, Virgin Galactic's latest grand ambition is, quite literally, to take us to the moon.

What about the notion of evangelism—the power to reach out and secure new acolytes? When Google rolled out its Gmail service, it attracted followers in a devilishly shrewd way. By making the service available by invitation only, Gmail became almost like a virtual religion; when a friend invited you to join its ranks, you felt as though you'd been welcomed into a semi-exclusive, lifelong community (it was only when they'd secured an estimated 10 million users that Gmail opened its doors to mere laymen). American Express had a similarly successful invitation-only strategy when it released its ultra-exclusive Centurion Black Card in the United States; tens of thousands of consumers called up asking to be placed on the short list. Doesn't every religion, and every brand, treat converts in a similar way, by making them feel honored to be members of its fold?

Symbols, too, are ubiquitous in most religions. The cross. A dove. An angel. A crown of thorns. Just as religions have their icons, so, too, do products and brands. And although, as we saw in Chapter 4, the logo is no longer as powerful as companies once believed, as the marketplace gets more and more crowded, certain simple yet powerful icons are increasingly taking hold, creating an instant global language, or shorthand. For example, every Apple icon—from the Apple logo itself, to its trash can, to the smiley face you see when you turn on the computer—is singularly associated with the company, even when it stands alone. Did you know that Apple today owns three hundred icons, and that Microsoft owns five hundred? Think about McDonald's unmistakable Golden Arches or Nike's signature "swoosh." (The story goes that the company commissioned a contractor to develop a number of logos, then asked customers to vote on which they liked best by ticking a box. Except, no one liked any of the logos, so in desperation, the founder ticked the only box with no accompanying logo—which from then on became the Nike "swoosh.") Far more so than the product logos, these symbols evoke powerful associations in us—whether it's athletic prowess or the promise of a juicy cheeseburger—in the same way that religious icons evoke powerful religious associations.

Remember seven-time Tour de France winner Lance Armstrong's 2004 "Live Strong" bracelet—that simple yellow wristband designed to raise money for cancer research and raise cancer awareness? Nike originally gave these away free of charge, but once the yellow silicone band became an icon for charitable giving, Armstrong's foundation ended up selling some $70 million worth, inspiring a slew of copycat bracelets that are now routinely handed out at everything from college tours to NFL football games to rock concerts.

Symbols like these can have an extremely powerful impact on why we buy. Think about Jimmy Buffett, the singer-songwriter who, in a woefully depressed music industry, is one of the few entertainers to consistently sell out his concerts year after year—in minutes, too, thanks to his millions of fans (who cheerfully refer to themselves as Parrotheads). It makes no difference that Jimmy Buffett and his band haven't had a hit record in years—fans still flock to his concerts. So what is this sixty-one-year-old tycoon selling, exactly? In a world where overworked people are handcuffed to computer screens and PDAs even when they're on vacation, Buffett and his best-known song "Margaritaville" have created a following that's founded on a handful of highly appealing symbols—sunshine, the ocean, relaxation, spring break, and rum drinks adorned with vivid little umbrellas. These symbols remind us that no matter how hectic our lives, we can all still let go, indulge our fantasies, and enjoy ourselves. It is a brand that Buffett has expanded with a chain of Margaritaville restaurants, books, and a successful satellite radio show.

Mystery, too, is a powerful force in religion. In religion, the unknown can be as powerful as the known—think of how many years scholars have spent pondering the mysteries of the Bible, or the ancient Shroud of Turin, or the Holy Chalice. When it comes to brands, mystery can be just as effective in attracting our attention. Coca-Cola, for example, draws on a sense of mystery with its secret formula—a mysterious yet distinctive recipe of fruit, oils, and spices that the company keeps in a safe-deposit box inside an Atlanta bank. The formula is so mysterious, in fact, that many schemes to obtain it have been attempted. In June 2005, an undercover agent pretending to be a high-ranking Pepsico representative met up with a man calling himself "Dirk" at Atlanta's Hartsfield-Jackson International Airport. "Dirk" was bearing an envelope containing Coca-Cola documents labeled "Classified: Confidential—Highly Restricted," as well as a sample of a new product that hadn't yet been released, and selling these secrets for a cool $1.5 million (tipped off by Pepsi, "Dirk" was later apprehended).

Another story goes that when Unilever was getting ready to launch a shampoo in Asia, a mischievous employee with time on his hands wrote on the label, just for the hell of it, *Contains the X9 Factor.* This last-minute addition went undetected by Unilever, and soon millions and millions of bottles of the shampoo were shipped to stores with those four words inscribed on the label. It would have cost too much to recall all the shampoo, so Unilever simply let it be. Six months later, when the shampoo had sold out, the company reprinted the label, this time leaving out the reference to the nonexistent "X9 Factor." To their surprise, they soon received a slew of outraged mail from their customers. None of the customers had any idea what the X9 Factor was, but were indignant that Unilever had dared to get rid of it. In fact, many people claimed that their shampoo wasn't working anymore, and that their hair had lost its luster, all because the company had dropped the elusive X9 Factor. It just goes to show that the more mystery and intrigue a brand can cultivate, the more likely it will appeal to us. Ever owned a Sony Trinitron? What the heck *is* a Trinitron, anyway? I'm supposedly the brand expert here, and I haven't the foggiest idea. I once asked a Sony executive what a Trinitron *did* exactly, and the response he gave me was so overinvolved that forty-five minutes later, I'd filtered out only a few scraps of it. Point is, whatever a Trinitron is, or does, it's still a mystery to me—but I want one more than ever.

In the past few years, there's even been a trend within the global cosmetics industry to create mystery around their brand by rolling out "scientific" formulas that claim to match scents with their wearer's DNA. Regardless of the fact that the notion of perfume matching a person's DNA is complete nonsense, it hasn't stopped any of these companies from trying to convince consumers that such mysterious formulas exist. Consider Chanel's new regenerating cream, Sublimage. "At the heart of Sublimage," the copy reads, "lies the quintessence of a unique active ingredient, Planifolia PFA, a true catalyst of cell renewal . . . now Sublimage has become a true skincare experience with the new Fluid and Mask PFA: Polyfactioning of Active Ingredients . . . A specific process developed by Chanel that allows for the creation of Planifolia PFA, an ultra-pure cosmetics active ingredient. Patent Pending."

I'm sorry, but what does any of this mean? It's crazy talk—but it's a mystery.

Ritual, superstition, religion—whether we're aware of it or not, all these factors contribute to what we think about when we buy. In fact, as the results of our brain-scan study would show, the most successful products are the ones that have the most in common with religion. Take Apple, for example, one of the most popular—and profitable—brands around.

I'll never forget the Apple Macromedia conference I attended in the mid-nineties. Sitting in a packed convention center in San Francisco among ten thousand cheering fans, I was surprised when Steve Jobs, the founder and CEO, ambled out onstage, wearing his usual monkish turtleneck, and announced that Apple was going to discontinue its Newton brand of handheld computers. Jobs then dramatically hurled a Newton into a garbage can a few feet away to punctuate his decision. Newton was done. Cooked.

In fury and desperation, the man next to me pulled out his

own Newton, threw it to the floor, and began furiously stomping on it. On the other side of me, a middle-aged man had begun to weep. Chaos was erupting in the Moscone Center! It was as though Jobs had announced that there would be no Second Coming after all. It occurred to me suddenly—as it would again, years later, when I paid a visit to the temple-like Apple store in midtown Manhattan and stood in awe as a slant of mid-morning light streamed in through the clear glass, beaming off the Bethlehem star–like Apple logo suspended by filament from the ceiling—that this wasn't any ordinary product demonstration. For its millions of fervent constituents, Apple wasn't just a brand, it was a *religion.*

NOW YOU MIGHT be thinking, this is all well and good, but is there scientific proof that brands have a great deal in common with spirituality and religion?

That's what my next brain-scan study would find out. It was the first time that anyone had tried to prove a scientific link between brands and the world's religions. And the results turned out to be as groundbreaking as the study itself.

For this portion of the study, I chose to examine the power of such powerful brand icons as Apple, Guinness, Ferrari, and Harley-Davidson, not just because they are popular brands, but because they were also what I refer to as "smashable" brands. "Smash Your Brand" is a phrase that goes back to 1915, when the Coca-Cola company asked a designer in Terre Haute, Indiana, to design a bottle that consumers could still recognize as a Coke bottle, even if it shattered into a hundred pieces.

Try smashing a brand yourself. Pick up that new, linen, lime-green, button-down Ralph Lauren shirt you just forked over $89.50 to buy. Since you can't physically smash fabric, take a pair of scissors and cut the shirt into a hundred little pieces. Hide the scrap with the polo pony on it. If you examine an individual piece, can you tell that Ralph Lauren manufactured the shirt? I doubt it. The quality of the linen fabric might indicate that what you're holding probably costs a lot more than an everyday brand, but without the pony, there's no way to tell whether your shirt was designed by Calvin Klein, Liz Claiborne, Perry Ellis, Tommy Hilfiger, or anyone else. (Once, when visiting a factory in China, I discovered that the factory tables were packed with one brand of clothing in the morning, another brand in the afternoon. The only difference: the cotton logo, which, as a finishing touch, workers placed carefully on each shirt, sweater, and hoodie, creating the sole, and staggering, price differential between branded shirts and unbranded ones.)

So why are products like Guinness, Ferrari, Harley-Davidson, and Apple "smashable"? Well, a few drops of Guinness are just as recognizably Guinness as a whole pint; the wheels of a Harley are as unmistakable as the bike itself; and a piece of scrap metal from a totaled Ferrari could be nothing else—thanks to its signature shade of red. And though it may make you wince to hurl that iPod against a brick wall, when you're gathering up the pieces, you'll know what "smashable" truly means. In fact, take a look at the front of your iPod right now. Do you see the Apple logo anywhere? I doubt it, because there isn't one. But yet, would you ever mistake it for any other brand? I doubt that, too.

I used smashable brands in this portion of the study because those are the brands that tend to be stronger and more emotionally engaging—in other words, they enjoy a passionate and loyal following. But in order to get a better picture of our relationship to strong brands, I knew I needed to assess our volunteers' response not just to strong brands, but to weak brands, too. So I included Microsoft, BP, and countless other brands sharing the same profile. Why these? Well, these are all brands that I consider to provoke limited or even negative emotional engagement among consumers. In other words, they leave most of us cold.

Regardless of whether we were showing our volunteers "strong" brands or "weak" ones, it was important that each was a leader within its category. That way, we could be sure that the results wouldn't be skewed by lesser or unknown brands.

Before our study got under way, we asked our sixty-five subjects to rate their spirituality from one to ten, with ten being the highest. Most termed their devoutness between seven and ten. This time around, we'd also narrowed down our volunteers to males, since we were combining our study with a related, and male-skewed, experiment: did sports, and sports heroes, activate the same areas of the brain as religions did? After all, just like members of religions, sports fans have a strong sense of belonging, usually to a hometown or favorite team; teams have a clear mission (to win); and, of course, a strong sense of us vs. them. Sports also offer a strong sensory appeal (think of the smell of a fresh-mown football field on game day, or the mouthwatering aroma of stadium hot dogs, or the sound of the national anthem played before the game begins). Few things seem grander than a championship title or a medal or a trophy, and stories and myths (the Curse of the

Bambino, for example) abound everywhere in the sports world. So I decided to compare how the brain responded to sports icons and sporting paraphernalia, compared with how they responded to religious imagery.

One by one, over the course of a few days, our volunteers filed into Dr. Calvert's lab and were hooked up to the fMRI machine. The room went dark and the images began to flicker past: A bottle of Coca-Cola. The Pope. An iPod. A can of Red Bull. Rosary beads. A Ferrari sports car. The eBay logo. Mother Teresa. An American Express card. The BP sign. A photograph of children praying. The Microsoft logo. Finally, images of selected teams and individuals from the worlds of football, soccer, cricket, boxing, and tennis. A church pew, followed by David Beckham, followed by a nun's habit, followed by the World Cup. And so on.

WHEN DR. CALVERT analyzed the fMRI data, she found that strong brands brought about greater activity in many areas of the brain involved in memory, emotion, decision-making, and meaning than weak brands did. This didn't surprise me terribly much. After all, it makes sense that an image of BP Oil would inspire less emotional engagement than a shiny red Ferrari.

But it was Dr. Calvert's next finding that was truly fascinating. She discovered that when people viewed images associated with the strong brands—the iPod, the Harley-Davidson, the Ferrari, and others—their brains registered the exact same patterns of activity as they did when they viewed the religious images. Bottom line, there was no discernible difference between the way the subjects' brains reacted to powerful brands and the way they reacted to religious icons and figures.

And, as it turns out, despite all that the world of sports has in common with major religions, even sports stars and sporting imagery didn't elicit quite as strong an emotional response in the brain as the strong and weak brands did. However, exposure to sports stars *did* activate the part of our brains associated with our sense of reward (the middle inferior orbitofrontal cortex) in a way that was similar to the patterns of arousal prompted by religious icons, suggesting that the feelings of reward associated with a victory on the soccer field were similar to the feelings of reward associated with, say, a moving church sermon or prayer.

Both strong and weak brands, however, were far more powerful than the sports imagery in stimulating the memory storage and decision-making regions of the brain. This makes intuitive sense; after all, when we're thinking about whether or not to buy a TV, a digital camera, or a new dress, our brains summon up all kinds of information about the product—its price, its features, our past experiences with it—and make a decision accordingly. When it comes to sports, though, there's little fact-finding or decision-making involved; we root for the Red Sox or the Indianapolis Colts because, well, we just *do.*

To sum up, our research showed that the emotions we (at least those of us who consider ourselves devout) experience when we are exposed to iPods, Guinness, and Ferrari sports cars are similar to the emotions generated by religious symbols such as crosses, rosary beads, Mother Teresa, the Virgin Mary, and the Bible. In fact, the reactions in our volunteers to the brands and religious icons were not just similar, they were almost identical. When these subjects viewed emotionally weaker brands, however, completely different areas of their brains were activated, suggesting that weaker brands didn't evoke the same associations.

Clearly, our emotional engagement with powerful brands (and to a lesser extent, sports) shares strong parallels with our feelings about religion. Which is why marketers and advertisers have begun to borrow even more heavily from the world of religion to entice us to buy their products. I've even seen evidence of this trend firsthand. Once, at a senior management meeting in Paris, a CEO of a major perfume company raised his hand. "Do we own any magic ingredients?" he asked his chief engineer. The engineer wrinkled his brow. "Uh, water?" he said at last. Pretty soon, the company had developed a "magic" ingredient and added it to the mix.

Lego was one of the first companies to infuse ritual and religion into their products. I was working for the company back then and had what I thought was a dazzlingly good idea to roll out a virtual advent calendar on the company Web site. Lego loved the idea; it was inexpensive and risk-free. Or so they thought. At which point the shit hit the fan. The first problem was a technical one—kids in New Zealand and Australia couldn't open the doors on the correct day, since they were twenty-four hours ahead of some parts of the world (we solved this glitch by hiring a Java programmer, who wrote a script for each user's nationality).

But the second problem, which turned out to be a much bigger one, is that advent calendars are specific to Christianity, and almost overnight, Lego was perceived as promoting a religious agenda. Thousands of angry e-mails from all over the world filled my company in-box—and I was the one responsible for responding to each one. I quickly learned that overt use of religion in advertising (as opposed to a more implicit, suggestive approach) not only didn't work, but could actually harm a legendary brand.

In Italy, the cell phone giant Vodafone will soon offer a service that beams daily quotations from Pope John Paul II via text message to subscribers' mobile phones. According to an article in the U.K. *Guardian,* Vodafone will also offer another text message service through which subscribers can receive a daily picture of a saint, accompanied by his or her most popular quotation.[4]

So do any other companies deliberately attempt to incorporate religious elements into their marketing? I'm sure they do, but I can all but guarantee you that in America at least, they won't ever admit it.

PUT RELIGION ASIDE now, and pretend you're shopping for a new TV. What makes you pick a Samsung over a Philips? Or, if you're in the mood for a snack, do you make an immediate beeline for the Triscuits over the Wheat Thins, the Chips Ahoy over the Pecan Sandies? And when you were shopping for cars last year, why wouldn't you consider anything but a Toyota? What's going on in your head?

In the next chapter, we'll be taking a look at a fascinating scientific discovery known as somatic markers, and how these "bookmarks of the brain" can affect how we choose one product over another. Which will lead us into an experiment involving one of the best-known—and most unanimously hated—sounds in the world, revealing a finding that left the marketing executives at Nokia flabbergasted.

7

The Power of Somatic Markers

PLAY ALONG WITH ME
for a moment as we head to the supermarket. Shouldn't take long; there are only a couple of items on our list.

Let's make our way to the peanut butter section first. There's Skippy, Peter Pan, Jif. The generic supermarket offering, plus a few virtuous organic brands—salt-free, no sugar added, the sort where the oil rises to the top.

Most consumers think about their choice for all of two seconds. In this case, let's say you grab the Jif, and we're on to our next stop.

Was your decision rational? It may have seemed that way to you as you made your choice, but it wasn't, not by a long shot. If your decision-making process was conscious—and articulated—my guess is it might have gone something like this: *I associate Skippy with childhood . . . it's been around forever, so I feel it's trustworthy . . . but isn't it laden with sugar and other preservatives I shouldn't be eating? . . . Same goes for Peter Pan, plus the name is so childish. And I'm not buying that generic brand. It costs 30 cents less, which makes me suspicious. In my experience, you get what you pay for... The organic stuff? Tasteless, the few times I had it... always needs salt, too... Plus, didn't I read somewhere that "organic" doesn't necessarily mean anything, plus it's almost double the price... Jif... what's that old advertising slogan of theirs: "Choosy Mothers Choose Jif"... Well, I am a fairly discriminating person...*

These are the subconscious conversations that go on in our heads every time we choose one product over another. Except they are rarely if ever uttered aloud. Instead, we rely on almost instant shortcuts that our brains have created to help us make buying decisions.

Our next stop is bottled water. There are dozens of glistening bottles, both glass and plastic, and in all shapes and sizes, too. Again, let's imagine the rational conversation that might take place inside your head as you decide which one to buy: *Dasani... no, that's the one Coke makes... Someone told me it was nothing more than tap water with a phony name... I don't want my bottled water to be "commercial," it should be special, chic... wait, what's this one? Iskilde. By far the most beautiful bottle on the shelf. From Denmark... No idea what Iskilde means, but isn't Denmark a land of snow and streams and healthy people on ski slopes? Even the lettering on the bottle is clear-blue, like Scandinavian eyes... The bottle is so clean and simple and icy-looking—like the water from a Danish mountain stream... Iskilde: it's almost like a Danish guy saying "It's Cold." It's expensive, too, which probably means it's special...*

And so Iskilde goes into your cart. You've never tasted the stuff, but your gut tells you you've made the right decision. If I asked you to describe how you came to your decision, you'd probably shrug and reply "Instinct," or "No reason," or "I just did." But the real rationale behind your choices was in fact built on a lifetime of associations—some positive, others negative—that you weren't consciously aware of. Because when we make decisions about what to buy, our brain summons and scans incredible amounts of memories, facts, and emotions and squeezes them into a rapid response—a shortcut of sorts that allows you to travel from A to Z in a couple of seconds, and that dictates what you just put inside your shopping cart. A recent study conducted by German brand and retail experts, Gruppe Nymphenberg, found that over 50 percent of all purchasing decisions by shoppers are made spontaneously—and therefore unconsciously—at the point of sale.

These brain shortcuts have another name: a somatic marker.

THE GREEK PHILOSOPHER Socrates once told his student Theaetetus to imagine the mind as a block of wax "on which we stamp what we perceive or conceive." Whatever is impressed upon the wax, Socrates said, we remember and know, provided the image remains in the wax, but "whatever is obliterated or cannot be impressed, we forget and do not know."[1] A metaphor so suggestive and widespread that we still say that an experience "made an impression."

Imagine for a moment that you're a six-year-old kid. You're just home from school and you're hungry, so you wander into the kitchen to see what that nice smell is that's coming from the stove. Opening the oven door, you spy a navy-blue Le Creuset pot. You begin to pull out the pot when you recoil backward, your fingertips stinging. You're in tears; your parents come running; and assuming your fingertips weren't too badly burned, a half hour later you're back playing with your trains, dinosaurs, or sharks.

The tenderness of your fingertips will vanish in a few days, but your mind isn't quite so lenient. It won't forgive what happened; certainly it won't ever forget it. Subconsciously, the neurons in your brain have just assembled an equation of sorts, one linking together the concepts of "oven" and "hot" and "fingertips" and "grill" and "excruciating pain." In sum, this chain-link of concepts and body parts and sensations creates what scientist Antonio Damasio calls a somatic marker—a kind of bookmark, or shortcut, in our brains. Sown by past experiences of reward and punishment, these markers serve to connect an experience or emotion with a specific, required reaction. By instantaneously helping us narrow down the possibilities available in a situation, they shepherd us toward a decision that we know will yield the best, least painful outcome. Long after we've passed our sixth year, we "know" whether or not it's right to kiss a hostess we barely know good-bye after a cocktail party, whether it's safe to dive into a lake, how we should approach that German shepherd, or that if we reach into an oven without a mitt on, our fingers will get burned. If someone asks us how or why we know that, most of us shrug—what a funny question—and chalk up our response to "instinct."

These same cognitive shortcuts are what underlie most of our buying decisions. Remember: it took you less than ten seconds to choose the Jif and the Iskilde, based on a completely unconscious series of flags in your brain that led you straight to an emotional reaction. All of a sudden, you "just knew" which brand you wanted, but were completely unaware of the factors—the shape of the product's container, childhood memories, its price, and a lot of other considerations—that led to your decision.

But somatic markers aren't simply a collection of reflexes from childhood or adolescence. Every day, we manufacture new ones, adding them to the bulging collection already in place. And the bigger our brain's collection of somatic markers, whether for shampoos, face creams, chewing gums, breath mints, potato chips, vodka bottles, shaving creams, deodorants, vitamins, shirts, pants, dresses, TVs, or video cameras, the more buying decisions we're able to make. In fact, without somatic markers we wouldn't be able to make any decisions at all—much less parallel park a car, ride a bike, flag a taxi, decide how much money to take out of the ATM machine, plug a lamp into an electrical socket without getting electrocuted, or take a burning casserole dish out of the oven.

For example, why do many consumers choose to buy an Audi over other cars with equally attractive designs, comparable safety ratings, and similar prices? It might very well have something to do with the company's slogan, *Vorsprung durch Technik.* Now, I strongly doubt many people outside of Germany or Switzerland know what this means (roughly, it translates to "progress and/or head start through technology"; U2 fans, of which I'm one, will note that Bono murmurs the phrase at the beginning of the song "Zooropa"). But that's not the point. Most people *will* guess correctly that the phrase is German. Our brains link together "automobile" with "Germany" with everything we've picked up over our lifetimes about top-of-the-line Teutonic car manufacturing. High standards. Precision. Consistency. Rigor. Efficiency. Trustworthiness. The result: we walk out of the showroom holding the keys to a new Audi. Why? We are rarely conscious of it, but the fact is that in a world teeming with cars that are for the most part indistinguishable, a somatic marker that connects Germany with technological excellence comes alive in our brain and ushers us toward a brand preference.

Or let's imagine that you're shopping for a digital camera. Even with the vast array of features—optical zoom, tony image processors, face detection gizmos, red-eye correctors—most of them look exactly the same. So why do you find yourself gravitating toward the ones that come from Japan? Once, back before Japan became a global leader in manufacturing technology, the words "Made in Japan" turned you off. You associated it with cheap kids' toys, gadgets that fell apart after fifteen minutes, and crummy, mass-marketed merchandise put together by people working in substandard conditions. But now anything Japanese seems to you a marvel of cutting-edge sophistication. Again, based purely on a series of unconscious markers, your mind has linked together Japan with technological excellence and you leave the store with a new Japanese camera under your arm.

This is all very well and good, but by now you might be wondering, how do these markers form? And do companies and advertisers work to deliberately create these in our brains? You bet. Take TV commercials. If you've ever shopped for tires, you know that they all look the same—Dunlop, Bridgestone, Goodyear—nothing but a mind-numbing ocean of black rubber. Yet you automatically make your way, say, to the store's Michelin section. You know you're making the right choice but you can't really articulate why. In truth, your brand preference has very little to do with the tires themselves, but instead with the somatic markers the brand has carefully created. Remember the cute baby Michelin once used in their advertising? Or what about the Michelin man, whose plump, round appearance suggests the protective padding of a well-made tire? And then there are the Michelin Guides, those slender, authoritative, high-end travel and food guides (which the company invented so that consumers would drive around in pursuit of the best restaurants—and thus purchase more tires). Point is, all these seemingly unrelated bookmarks deliberately forge certain associations—safety for your child passengers; sturdy, reliable durability; and a high-quality, top-of-the-line, European experience. And it's these powerful associations that come together to shepherd you toward a choice that feels rational, but that isn't at all.

Professor Robert Heath, a British consultant who among other things has written extensively about somatic markers, has examined the success of a brand of British toilet paper known as Andrex that outsells its nearest rival, Kleenex, in the United Kingdom by an almost two-to-one margin. Both companies spend the same amount of money on TV ads, both are of equally high quality, and both cost approximately the same. Heath's explanation for Andrex's success? A small Labrador puppy. But what, pray tell, does a little dog have to do with an eight-pack of toilet paper?

For years, Andrex has used its puppy mascot to advertise how "soft, strong, and very long" its toilet paper is. In a series of commercials, the puppy is seen skidding down a snowy hill on a sheet of toilet paper; in another, a woman holds the puppy while behind them a long lacy banner of Andrex toilet paper billows and flutters behind a speeding car. At first, the connection between puppies and toilet paper seems obscure, kind of random. But as Heath writes, "Puppies are linked with growing young families; puppies are even linked to toilet training. The connections between any of these concepts and the puppy associations can be created and reinforced every time the ads are seen." Heath adds, "When faced with the need to buy toilet paper, the average consumer will not stop and try to recall the ads to mind. However, when they tap into their intuitive feelings about the two brands, the likelihood is that they will come up with a far richer set of conceptual links for Andrex than for Kleenex . . . All they might do is 'feel' that Andrex is somehow indefinably 'better' than Kleenex."[2]

For advertisers, it's easy and inexpensive to create a somatic marker in consumers' brains. Let's take an example from real life. How do you know to look both ways when you cross the street? Chances are you once had a close call that came as a shock—and that shock has stuck with you ever since. Since somatic markers are typically associations between two incompatible elements—in this case, an uneventful morning and a sudden screech of brakes—they are far more memorable, and lasting, than other associations we form throughout our lives. Which is why, in attempting to hook our attention, advertisers aim to create surprising, even shocking associations between two wildly disparate things.

Take a guy by the name of Tom Dickson. Tom Dickson resembles any midwestern, middle-aged suburban dad. But this suburban dad has a rather out-of-the-ordinary job. He sells blenders. But that's not what's most bizarre about him. To advertise the blenders, he has created a series of short videos, available on the Blendtec Blender Web site (which have migrated virally over to YouTube), which open with the question "Will it blend?"—a concept likely borrowed from Dan Aykroyd's famous *Saturday Night Live* skit, in which he used a blender to pulverize a sea bass. As viewers look on saucer-eyed, Tom Dickson proceeds to grind, chop, mash, mince, puree, and annihilate a series of objects inside his kitchen blender. Bic lighters. A tiki torch. A length of garden hose. Three hockey pucks. Even an Apple iPhone. Every week, Tom Dickson makes it his mission to pulverize something new and seemingly unpulverizable.

Watching an iPhone whirl and clack until it's been reduced to a smoking mass of black particles is, to say the least, un-forgettable. It creates a somatic marker so dramatic in our brains that the next time we're whipping up a strawberry smoothie, we can't help but think: wouldn't the Blendtec Blender do a better job? Our brains associate the brand of blender with the memorable image of an iPhone being ground into a steaming pile of dust, and without even con-sciously realizing it, we've picked up the Blendtec box.[3]

Sony created an ingenious somatic marker in the weeks be-fore the release of *Spiderman 3,* using men's rooms in selected theaters. A guy would stroll in and see a conventional line of urinals and stalls. Nothing out of the ordinary. That is, until he would happen to gaze upward and see a single stand-alone plastic urinal seven feet above his head. Next to it: the words *Spiderman 3 . . . Coming Soon.* Pretty memorable, huh?

And remember the Energizer Bunny? "Nothing outlasts the Energizer. He keeps going and going and going..." A stuffed pink creature banging down on a drum, marching across dinner tables, knocking over bottles of wine. Impossi-bly irritating. Also impossibly hard not to associate with long-lasting power when you're browsing the battery section.

Fifteen years ago, when I was living in Copenhagen and working for an advertising agency, Luciano Pavarotti paid his first visit to Denmark. It was a huge deal, and the Danes were beside themselves. Everything was in place to celebrate his arrival—gala dinners, special broadcasts, interviews, and open-air broadcasts. But at the very last minute, the tenor canceled his performance, having come down with a sore throat. I don't think I've ever witnessed a nationwide disappointment like that. I was worried the entire country would have to go on Prozac.

But it gave my advertising team and me an idea. In less than a few hours, we managed to convince a sore-throat lozenge manufacturer named GaJol to buy space in newspapers and magazines with a new tagline: *If only Pavarotti had known about GaJol.* It turned a nationwide disaster into a coup for the company. Even fifteen years later, many Danes associate GaJol lozenges with the beloved opera singer. Just goes to show that somatic markers are hard to erase.

Another time, when I was visiting Eastern Europe, I sat next to the CEO of one of the region's largest banks. How, he asked me, could he boost his bank's awareness? Now, I'd just polished off a large meal and a number of glasses of wine, and that probably contributed to my spontaneously advising him to paint his entire bank—and everything in it—pink. The fact that banks and pink don't go together is exactly why I thought it would work. Six months later, he e-mailed me. He'd done as I'd said. Every branch, every car, every staff uniform, even his tie, was pink—but everyone hated it. What should he do? Stick with it, I said, and in three months you'll notice a difference. Approximately ninety days later, he e-mailed me again. Now that customers had begun to associate the bank's pink with the comfort and security of a childhood piggy bank, the bank had the highest brand awareness of any bank in the country and had cut their marketing costs in half.

SOME ADVERTISERS CREATE somatic markers in consumers' minds using humor. In an ad for Lamisil, a pill used for foot infection, a yellow-bodied cartoon-like gremlin approaches a set of toes, lifts up one of the big toes and hops underneath, where he's soon joined by his cronies—that is, until the owner of the foot pops a Lamisil. By anthropomorphizing germs in a humorous and memorable way this ad creates a powerful somatic marker that links the brand to powerful germ-fighting.[4]

Because somatic markers are based on past experiences of reward and punishment, fear too can create some of the most powerful somatic markers, and many advertisers are all too happy to take advantage of our stressed-out, insecure, increasingly vulnerable natures. Practically every brand category I can think of plays on fear, either directly or indirectly. We're sold medicines to ward off depression, diet pills and gym memberships to prevent obesity, creams and ointments to quiet fears of aging, and even computer software to ward off the terror of our hard drives crashing. I predict that in the near future advertising will be based more and more on fear-driven somatic markers, as advertisers attempt to scare us into believing that *not* buying their product will make us feel less safe, less happy, less free, and less in control of our lives.

For a fear-driven somatic marker, it's worth looking at Johnson's No More Tears Baby Shampoo. What does it evoke? Fear of the same thing it promises to help you avoid: tears. Memories of stinging red eyes, from childhood onward. I got shampoo in my eyes recently, and guess what? It *still* hurts like hell, at any age. Similarly, I recently ran across an ad for Colgate toothpaste claiming that "emerging scientific research is associating serious gum disease with other diseases such as heart disease, diabetes and stroke." In short, brush with Colgate—or else you'll die!

Or what about attention deficit disorder, and the litany of negative, even catastrophic associations it carries? Fifteen years ago, it barely existed, but today it's being diagnosed left, right, and sideways. I'm not suggesting that some kids don't have it, or can't benefit from treatment, but ADD (and the fear of our children being diagnosed with it) has saturated our culture like a virus. And the result, of course, is millions of parents buying their children drugs. A parent's internal monologue may go something like this: *If my child doesn't take Ritalin or Adderal or Concerta, he won't be able to concentrate in school. He'll fall behind. His grades will suffer. He'll be marginalized by his peers. He'll begin hanging out with other low-performing kids. He won't get into college. He'll drift from job to job. He may even end up in jail. All because I didn't address his ADD when he was in kindergarten.* Fear, in my experience, spreads faster than anything else—and the ads for those drugs have done a very nice job scaring the pants off us.

Of course, not all somatic markers are based on pain and fear. Some of the most effective ones are rooted in sensory experiences, which in fact can often be quite pleasant. So in the next part of our study, we're going to take on the power of the senses in our everyday buying decisions. In a revolutionary experiment, we'll put somatic markers under an fMRI—and show how one of the most famous sounds in the world can completely destroy an otherwise beloved brand.

8

A SENSE OF WONDER

Selling to Our Senses

LET'S TAKE A STROLL
around Times Square. We'll pretend we're tourists, necks craned, eyes drawn irresistibly upward as we ogle the oversized billboards that seem to block out every piece of sky. Red neon news and business tickertapes wrapping around the buildings, twenty-foot-high billboards of men in underwear, women in pink lingerie, oversized bottles of perfume and tequila and diamond-encrusted wristwatches for the well-heeled modern man and woman. Not to mention the phantasmagoric blur of logos, everything from Virgin Records to Starbucks to Skechers to Maxell to Yahoo!. And the same visual assault is taking place in downtown Tokyo, London, Hong Kong, and every other commercial mecca across the world. But what if I told you that much of this visual, in-your-face advertising is, on the part of advertisers, a largely wasted effort? That, in fact, our visual sense is far from our most powerful in seducing our interest and getting us to buy. What if I could prove to you that when working alone, our eyes—

the same ones sneaking a glance at that Nordic god in his skivvies, that petulant beauty in her bikini bottom, that decanter of Chanel, those flashing letters spelling out Swatch, JVC, Planet Hollywood, AT&T, Chase Manhattan, McDonald's, Taco Bell, T-Mobile, and so on—are in fact much less potent than we have long believed?

Today, we are more visually overstimulated than ever before. And in fact, studies have shown that the more stimulated we are, the harder it is to capture our attention.

A brain-scanning company called Neuroco has carried out a study for 20th Century Fox that measured subjects' electrical brain activity and eye movement in response to commercials placed inside a video game. During a virtual stroll through Paris, volunteers viewed ads on billboards, bus stop shelters, and the sides of buses to see which best got their attention. The results: none of them. The researchers found that all the visual saturation resulted only in glazed eyes, not higher sales.

I'm not denying that sight is a crucial factor in why we buy. But as our two upcoming tests would show, sight in many cases isn't as powerful as we first assumed—and smell and sound are substantially more potent than anyone had ever dreamed of. In fact, in a wide range of categories (not just the obvious, like food), sound and smell can be even stronger than sight. And this was the impetus that lay behind the experiment Dr. Calvert and I carried out—the first-ever full-scale study of its kind—to test the enormous (and never before acknowledged) role of our senses in why we buy what we do.

As I've mentioned, advertisers have long assumed that the logo is *everything*. Companies have spent thousands of hours and millions of dollars creating, tweaking, altering, and testing their logos—and making sure those logos are in our faces, above our heads, and tattooed beneath our feet. That's because marketers have long focused on driving and motivating consumers visually. But the truth of the matter is, visual images are far more effective, and more memorable, when they are coupled with another sense—like sound or smell. To fully engage us emotionally, companies are discovering, they'd be better off not just inundating us with logos, but pumping fragrances into our nostrils and music into our ears as well.

It's called Sensory Branding™.

FOR THE FIRST of two related experiments on brands and our senses, our volunteers would be testing two experimental fragrances on behalf of a well-known fast-food restaurant chain—let's call it Pete's—and choosing which fragrance best complemented a certain menu item.

Over the course of the next month, Dr. Calvert and her team exposed our twenty study subjects to images (including logos) and fragrances of four well-known brands. First the images and fragrances were presented individually, and then at the same time. These included Johnson & Johnson's No More Tears Baby Shampoo, Dove soap, a frosty, ice-filled glass of Coca-Cola, as well as an assortment of images and aromas associated with Pete's and their global chain of fast-food restaurants. By pressing a button on their hand consoles, our volunteers could control the onset of the images and fragrances, and rate the appeal of what they were viewing and smelling on a nine-point scale, ranging from very unpleasant to very pleasant.

After crunching the data, Dr. Calvert discovered that for the most part, when our volunteers were presented with the images and the fragrances individually, they found them equally pleasant to look at as to smell, suggesting that we as consumers are equally seduced by the sight of a product as by its scent. However, when Dr. Calvert presented the images and fragrances at the same time, she found that, in general, subjects rated the image-fragrance combinations to be more appealing than either the image or the fragrance alone. And, even more intriguingly, when Dr. Calvert presented our volunteers with the first of Pete's two experimental fragrances along with an image of a product that seemed incongruous with the smell—say a picture of a Dove soap bar along with the fragrance of scorched canola oil—the "pleasantness" quotient dropped, because the image and the fragrance didn't match up.

The other image-fragrance combination, on the other hand, went over like gangbusters. Just imagine viewing a fish-filet sandwich along with the slightest whiff of lemon, perhaps evoking that summer you spent grilling fresh fish on the beaches of Cape Cod or the Hamptons. Much more pleasant, right? That's because this time around the sight and smell of the product were congruous—a perfect collaboration between the eyes and the nose.

So what is going on in our brains that makes us prefer certain image/smell combinations over others? As Dr. Calvert explained, when we see and smell something we like at the same time—like Johnson & Johnson's Baby Powder combined with its signature vanilla-y scent—various regions of our brains light up in concert. Among them is the right medial orbitofrontal cortex, a region associated with our perception of something as pleasant or likable. But in cases where a brand matches up poorly with a fragrance—say, Johnson's Baby Shampoo combined with an odor of root beer—there's activation in the left lateral orbitofrontal cortex, a region of the brain connected to aversion and repulsion, which is why our subjects responded so unfavorably to the incongruous combinations. What's more, when we are exposed to combinations that seem to go together, the right piriform cortex (which is our primary olfactory cortex) and the amygdala (which encodes emotional relevance) are both activated. So in other words, when a pleasant fragrance matches up with an equally appealing and congruous visual image, we not only perceive it as more pleasant, we're also more likely to remember it, but if the two are incongruous, forget about it. Literally.

But it was Dr. Calvert's last finding that amazed me the most. On the basis of our sight-and-smell experiment, she concluded that *odor* activates many of the exact same brain regions as the *sight* of a product—even the sight of that product's logo. In short, if you smell a doughnut, you're likely to picture it in your head—along with that Dunkin' Donuts or Krispy Kreme logo. Smell that signature Abercrombie scent? The letters spelling A-B-E-R-C-R-O-M-B-I-E & F-I-T-C-H will flash like a Broadway marquee behind your forehead. So while companies are spending billions of dollars a year saturating our sidewalks, our airwaves, and everyplace else with logos, they'd do just as well in capturing our interest—if not better—by appealing to our sense of smell instead.

How, though, can smell activate some of the same areas of the brain as vision? Again, chalk it up to mirror neurons. If you catch a whiff of French Roast in the morning, chances are good your brain can "see" a cup of Maxwell House coffee on your kitchen counter. Thanks to mirror neurons, sound, too, can evoke equally powerful visual images. In my lectures, I often ask audiences to close their eyes. After tearing a piece of paper in two, I ask them what just happened. "You just ripped a piece of paper in two," they murmur, their eyes still shut. It's not just that they recognized the sound of ripping paper; they were actually visualizing me rip the paper in half.

As you can see, our senses are incredibly important in helping us interpret the world around us, and in turn play a critical role in our behavior. Play-Doh, Johnson & Johnson's Baby Powder—take a whiff of either of these products and more likely than not, you'll be transported (for better or for worse) back to your childhood. Once when I was giving a lecture, I asked a male member of the audience to sniff a red Crayola crayon. He promptly burst into tears. I asked him gently why he was crying. He told me, and the thousand other people in the room, that as a child, every time he was caught drawing his dream car using his Crayolas, the teacher used to punish him by rapping his knuckles with a ruler. It was the first time he'd smelled a Crayola since. Believe me, that's the very last time I ambush a stranger with a crayon.

If you had to guess, what would you expect one of the most recognized and best-liked fragrances all over the world to be? Chocolate? Lilacs? Money? Try Johnson's Baby Powder, a scent that's beloved everywhere from Nigeria to Pakistan to Saudi Arabia. (Yet practically no one can remember the Johnson & Johnson's logo.) Why Johnson & Johnson's Baby Powder? The power of sensory association. No matter how old you are, if you take a whiff of Johnson & Johnson's Baby Powder, chances are good that all those primal childhood associations will be reignited in your memory. Being fed by your mother. What it felt like to be held in her arms. These kinds of associations are why some companies use the scent of vanilla—which is found in breast milk (and, not coincidentally, is the most popular scent in the United States)—in their products. Why do you think Coca-Cola chose to roll out Coca-Cola Vanilla and Black Cherry Vanilla Coke lines over any other variety of flavors they could have created? In fact, the scent of vanilla is so appealing, one experiment carried out in a local clothing store in the Pacific Northwest showed that when "feminine scents" such as vanilla were sprayed in the women's clothing sections, sales of female apparel actually doubled.[1]

Of all our senses, smell is the most primal, the most deeply rooted. It's how our ancestors developed a taste for food, sought out mates, and intuited the presence of enemies. When we smell something, the odor receptors in our noses make an unimpeded beeline to our limbic system, which controls our emotions, memories, and sense of well-being. As a result, our gut response is instantaneous. Or as Pam Scholder Ellen, a Georgia State University marketing professor, puts it, "All of our other senses, you think before you respond, but with scent, your brain responds before you think."[2] And though smell preferences vary across cultures (Indians, for example, love sandalwood) and generations (if you were born before 1930, chances are you're fond of fresh-mown grass and horses, whereas if you were born after that, synthetic fragrances such as Play-Doh and even Sweet Tarts likely appeal to you), they are all shaped, to some extent, by our innate associations.[3]

So I suppose it's not surprising that it hasn't taken long for smart marketers to tack on fragrance to products they are selling. Samsung's flagship electronics store in New York City smells like honeydew melon, a light signature fragrance intended to relax consumers and put them in a South Sea–island frame of mind—maybe so they don't flinch at the prices. Thomas Pink, the British clothier, was once well known for pumping its U.K. stores full of the scent of freshly laundered cotton. British Airways wafts a fragrance known as Meadow Grass into the stale air of its business lounges to try to simulate the feeling of being outdoors, rather than in a stuffy airport. And both peanut butter and Nescafé jars are carefully designed to release the maximum amount of fragrance the moment their lids come off (for Nescafé, this took some tweaking, since freeze-dried coffee by itself doesn't smell like much).

Ever walked into a fast-food restaurant with the intention of ordering the virtuous, artery-friendly iceberg-lettuce salad, but ended up going for the triple-bacon cheeseburger with a side of large fries instead? It was that smell that got you, right? Fresh, juicy, charcoal-y, that seductive aroma seemed to suffuse every pore in your body. You were powerless to resist it.

But that smell you're inhaling comes not from a hot, smoking grill but from a spray canister with a name like RTX9338PJS—code name for the "just-cooked-bacon-cheeseburger-like-fragrance" that the fast-food restaurant was pumping through its vents. Mmm—makes me hungry just thinking about it.

Speaking of food, do you know why most modern supermarkets now have bakeries so close to the store entrance? Not only does the fragrance of just-baked bread signal freshness and evoke powerful feelings of comfort and domesticity, but store managers know that when the aroma of baking bread or doughnuts assails your nose, you'll get hungry—to the point where you just may discard your shopping list and start picking up food you hadn't planned on buying. Install a bakery, and sales of bread, butter, and jam are almost guaranteed to increase. In fact, the whiff of baking bread has proven a profitable exercise in increasing sales across many product lines. Some Northern European supermarkets don't even bother with actual bakeries; they just pump artificial fresh-baked-bread smell straight into the store aisles from ceiling vents.

Even the subtlest of aromas can have a potent effect on us as shoppers. In a 2005 study, two researchers placed a barely discernible lemon-scented cleaning liquid in a bucket of warm water concealed behind a wall. Half the volunteers unknowingly took their seats in the scented room; the other half plopped themselves down in an unscented room. Then the participants were asked to write down what they planned to do that day. Thirty-six percent of the participants in the scented room listed an activity that related to cleaning, compared to only 11 percent of the people in the unscented room. Next, the authors asked a fresh set of twenty-two college students to fill out an unrelated questionnaire in either the scented or the unscented room. They were then moved to a different room, where they were given an extremely messy, crumbly cookie to eat. Hidden cameras observed that those who had been seated in the scented room made less of a mess—merely smelling the cleanser made the people in the scented room more fastidious in their eating. Yet when questioned afterward, not one of the subjects was remotely aware of the influence of scent on their behavior.[4]

In another study carried out by Dr. Alan Hirsch, researchers placed two identical pairs of Nike running shoes in two separate but identical rooms. One room was pumped full of a light floral scent; the other wasn't. Volunteers examined the running shoes in each room, then filled out questionnaires. By 84 percent, subjects preferred the running shoes they'd looked at in the florally scented room. Moreover, they assessed the scented Nikes as costing roughly $10 more than the pairs in the unscented room. In a related experiment in Germany, the fragrance of freshly cut grass was sprayed into a home improvement store. From the second the pumps started emitting the grassy mist, 49 percent of all customers surveyed before and after claimed that the staff appeared to be more knowledgeable about the store's products.

And sensory branding is becoming more and more common. A California convenience store chain has experimented with wafting a fresh coffee smell into its parking lots to lure customers inside its stores. Procter & Gamble recently rolled out Puffs facial tissue tinged with the scent of Vicks, attempting to play on consumers' childhood memories of their mothers' treating their colds with Vicks' ointment.[5] Americhip, a leading manufacturer that manages to integrate multisensory technologies into magazine ads and print collateral for today's leading global advertisers, produced an ad for Diet Pepsi that contained sound, taste, and pop-up features. Reader awareness of this three-pronged ad in *People* magazine? One hundred percent—for the first time in the magazine's history. And in conjunction with the BRAND sense agency, Britain's Royal Mail has begun developing a program to enhance their marketing mailings with aromas and flavors. Tear open a flyer from a shampoo company, and through "microencapsulation"—a process that allows a scent to be released when you open an envelope—a fresh shampoo smell will all of a sudden envelop you like a cloud.

How to escape this assault on our noses? By checking into a hotel? Sorry, you're out of luck. Both the Hyatt Park Vendôme and the original Hyatt chains have suffused their rooms and lobbies with their own signature fragrances; the latter even infuses the smell of the macaroons they serve at their restaurants.

Of course, experiments involving fragrance can backfire. In 2006, San Francisco bus shelters equipped with cookie-scent-infused strips for a "Got Milk?" campaign had to be scrapped thirty-six hours later when commuters complained that the smell of chocolate chips and cookie batter was triggering allergic reactions.[6]

And Johnson & Johnson and Play-Doh have played around with their fragrances so much that they've lost the original formulas. In Europe, at least, Johnson & Johnson can no longer re-create its exact original recipe (their competitors' fragrances smell more like the original Johnson & Johnson's Baby Powder than Johnson & Johnson's own signature scent). And when I once contacted Play-Doh to see if I could secure the original smell, I was told that the company has never been able to replicate the original fragrance; they're only about 80 percent there. Sad for us, annoying for them.

CLEARLY, SMELL IS very closely tied to how we experience brands or products. Is the same true of touch? In his best-selling book *Why We Buy,* retail guru Paco Underhill writes about the critical importance of touching clothing before we buy it. We like to stroke, rub, caress, and run our fingers through the garments we're considering before we commit to buying them—kind of like a sensory test run. Why do you think those tables of clothing at the Gap and Banana Republic are positioned where they are? To be looked at? Of course not. They're there awaiting your fingers.

Or, take electronics. In general, we like our gadgets to be small, compact, and lightweight—James Bond–style. Irrationally, we conclude that the tinier and lighter our digital camera or tape recorder is, the more intricate and cutting-edge the technology inside it must be. Often that's true, up to a point. Certain companies, however, would argue that the heavier a product, the better its quality. A Bang & Olufsen remote control, for example, would weigh perhaps half of what it does if it wasn't stuffed with a completely useless wad of aluminum to make customers believe they're holding something substantial, sturdy, and worthy of the high price. Once, to prove a point, I conducted a test. I gave one hundred consumers two Bang & Olufsen remote controls, one with aluminum inside, the other without it. The immediate reaction from the consumers to the lighter-weight remote? "It's broken." All because of the lack of weight. Even when they found out the lightweight one was completely functional, they still felt its quality was inferior. Or what about Duracell's intriguing idea to design batteries shaped like bullets (the product unfortunately never hit the shelves). Research showed that when men who replaced the normal batteries in their flashlights with the heavy bullet-shaped ones (a process which felt not unlike loading a gun) were asked whether they thought the new batteries were more powerful than traditional ones, every single man answered yes—despite the fact that the bullet design actually substantially weakened the power of the battery. My point? Whether you prefer your gadgets stuffed with metal, light as air, or heavy as ammo, the feel of a product plays an important role in whether we decide to buy it.

A FEW YEARS back, I traveled to Saudi Arabia on an assignment to brand eggs. Yes, you read that right—eggs. After touching down in Jeddah, a car picked me up and drove into the middle of the 125-degree Fahrenheit Saudi Arabian desert. Two and a half hours later, I found myself standing inside one of the largest egg farms in the world.

My hosts had ferried me out into the desert to advise them on how to create eggs that would most appeal to the visual senses. It would seem a slightly bizarre request, until you realize how many varieties of eggs there are in the world and how much the appearance of eggs has to do with which type we select. For a long time, white eggs were popular among consumers, who associated them with cleanliness, good hygiene, and high standards. Then, gradually—no one knows why exactly—the public had a change of heart. Suddenly white was out, brown was in. It seemed consumers perceived brown eggs as more organic, more natural. But that still left manufacturers with the problem of what to do about the insides of eggs.

A general rule of thumb of the egg industry is that the more yellow a yolk appears, the more it will appeal to consumers. It's instinctual—probably an evolutionary adaptation that kept our ancestors from eating bad eggs. At any rate, when you add coloring to chicken food, color migrates into the cells of the egg yolk, so egg farmers can enhance the hue of their egg yolks by adding coloring to the grain. My job was to help this company create the perfect yellow. For ethical reasons, I couldn't support the idea of adding artificial coloring to the grain, so instead, I identified a vitamin mixture that could be added to the hens' feed that would produce yolks from light yellow to middling-yellow to the passionate yellow, plus all the variations in between.

So the next time you sit down for breakfast in your local diner, and the waiter sets two fried eggs with gorgeously yellow yolks in front of you, well, I plead guilty.

My point is, colors can be very powerful in connecting us emotionally to a brand. A few years ago, I conducted another little test. I invited six hundred women into a room, and presented each of them with a blue Tiffany's box. There was nothing inside, I have to admit, but they didn't know that. When the women received the box, we measured their heart rate and blood pressure. And guess what? Their heart rates went up 20 percent, like that. The women never saw the logo, just the color—with its powerful associations with engagement, marriage, babies, and fertility.

Perhaps for this same reason, the color pink, with its associations of luxury, sensuality, and femininity, is used to sell everything from sleepwear, underwear, perfume and soaps, to drugstore remedies (got an upset stomach? Pepto-Bismol will neutralize and soothe your indigestion) to toys to computers. That's right, thanks to the unexpected success of a pink laptop manufactured by the Hong Kong company VTech, marketers from Toys "R" Us to the NFL, the NHL and NASCAR are starting to roll out pink versions of their best-selling toys and sports clothing.

Color gets our buying juices going in other ways, too. When Heinz rolled out its EZ Squirt Blastin' Green ketchup in 2001, customers bought more than 10 million bottles of the stuff in its first seven months on the market, the highest sales spike in the brand's history—all because of a simple color change. And when Apple announced "It doesn't have to be beige" in the weeks before they rolled out their candy-colored iMacs (the iMacs and their distinctively childlike colors were in fact literally inspired by candy; Steve Jobs later stated half-jokingly that he wanted people to "lick them"), people started preordering them like crazy. In a study of phone directory advertising, researchers found that colored ads hold customers' attention for two seconds or more, whereas black-and-white images hold our interest for less than one second—a crucial difference in the retail world, when you consider the fact that on average, most products have only one-twentieth of a second to grab our attention before we move on.

A study carried out by the Seoul International Color Expo found that color goes so far as to increase brand recognition by up to 80 percent. When asked to approximate the importance of color when buying products, 84.7 percent of total respondents claimed that color amounted to more than half the criterion they consider when they're choosing a brand. Other studies have shown that when people make a subconscious judgment about a person, environment, or product within ninety seconds, between 62 and 90 percent of that assessment is based on color alone.

A decade ago, when I was working for BBDO, I developed a "choose a new color" ad campaign for M&Ms in Europe. Back then, blue, pink, and white M&Ms didn't exist, so we asked consumers, via the Web, which color they would most like to have melt in their mouths (not in their hands). In the end they picked blue, and sure enough when Mars rolled out the new color, sales rose.[7] Another time, Mercedes-Benz asked my team to create a new Web site for their fleet of high-end automobiles. So we created a riotously colorful Web site that consumers seemed to love (though the company hated it enough to discontinue it).

Even though sight is not as powerful in getting us to buy as we once believed, much of what we perceive every day is connected to our eyesight. Still, most of the time, we're barely aware of it. Consider a fascinating study by a major French food manufacturer testing two different prototype containers for a diet mayonnaise product aimed at female shoppers. Both containers held the exact same mayo and bore the exact same label. The only difference: the shapes of the bottles. The first was narrow around the middle, and thicker at the top and on the bottom. The second had a slender neck that tapered down into a bulbous bottom, like a genie bottle. When asked which product they preferred, every single subject—all diet-conscious females—selected the first bottle without even having tasted the stuff. Why? The researchers concluded that the subjects were associating the shape of the bottle with an image of their own bodies. And what woman wants to resemble an overstuffed Buddha, particularly after she's just spread diet mayonnaise on her turkey and alfalfa sandwich?

AS FOR SOUND? Well, believe it or not, sound branding has been around since the 1950s. General Electric, for example, created its familiar three-chime sound—the auditory equivalent of a logo—decades ago. Kellogg's, too, has spent many years cultivating a signature sound, even going so far as to hire a Danish lab to design a one-of-a-kind *crunch*, so that any child would be able to hear the difference between the sound of eating generic cornflakes and the Kellogg's brand. And at Bahlsen, a German food company, a development team of 16 researchers works diligently to engineer its own optimal *crunch* for its biscuits and potato chips. They don't take their jobs lightly, either. The biting and chewing noises are transmitted via speakers into the research lab, where they're continuously analyzed, enhanced, and perfected.

More recently, the Ford Motor Company created a new latch system for their Tauruses that makes a recognizable vaultlike sound when the doors close.[8] Did you know that the sound a jar of freeze-dried coffee or a can of Pringles potato chips makes when opened is largely engineered to make you associate the product with lip-smacking freshness? What about the tick-tick-tick of your iPod wheel, or the unmistakable chiming sound it makes when you turn it on and off? Or what about the sounds associated with McDonald's? After the racket of screaming kids, the sounds most associated with the fast food chain are the beep-beep-beep the french fry machine makes when the fries are ready and the scratchy punching sound your straw makes when it penetrates the plastic soda cup. Can you hear it right now? Bet you can, and it's making you crave an ice cold Coke and a large fries.

And of course, nothing sticks in the head like a jingle, no matter how idiotic or downright obnoxious it is. What about this one: "I'm a Pepper, he's a Pepper, she's a Pepper, we're a Pepper; wouldn't you like to be a Pepper, too?" (Dr Pepper). Or the classic "Plop, plop, fizz, fizz—oh, what a relief it is"

(Alka-Seltzer). Consider the Meow Mix jingle. How many times have you gotten that simple "Meow-meow-meow-meow-meow-meow-meow-meow-meow" lodged in your head?

Not convinced of the power of sound? Consider the fact that classical music has been found to deter vandalism, loitering, and even violent crime in Canadian parks, 7-Eleven parking lots, and subways. Figures released in 2006 showed that when classical music was piped over loudspeakers in the London Underground, robberies dropped by 33 percent, assaults on staff by 25 percent, and vandalism of trains and stations by 37 percent.[9]

Sound can even determine whether we pick up a bottle of French Chardonnay over a German Riesling. Over a two-week period, two researchers at the University of Leicester played either accordion-heavy, recognizably French music or a German Bierkeller brass band over the speakers of the wine section inside a large supermarket. On French music days, 77 percent of consumers bought French wine, whereas on Bierkeller music days, the vast majority of consumers made a beeline for the German section of the store. In short, a customer was three to four times more likely to select a bottle of wine that they associated with the music playing overhead than one they didn't. Were customers aware of what they were hearing? No doubt they were, peripherally. But only one out of the forty-four customers who agreed to answer a few questions at the checkout counter mentioned it among the reasons they bought the wine they did.[10]

And the cable channel A&E recently proved the power of sound in advertising by erecting a "sonic" billboard in New York City to promote a new paranormal-themed television series. Broadcasting from two oversized rooftop speakers, disembodied voices hissed "What's that?," "Who's there?," and "It's not your imagination" at startled pedestrians.[11] Creepy as hell, but it got people talking—and watching.

The point is, sounds trigger strong associations and emotions and can exert a powerful influence on our behavior. Which brings us to our second sensory experiment: what happens when a brand is incredibly popular yet is associated with a well-known signature sound that leaves people cold?

WITH ROUGHLY 400 million cell phones in circulation and a 2007 market share of 40 percent,[12] Nokia is one of the most popular brands in the world. As a result, most of us are familiar with the communication giant's famous and unmistakable signature ring tone. Twenty percent of all Nokia subscribers keep the company's default ring tone (the one that played such a prominent part in the hit movie *Love Actually*), and if prompted, 41 percent of all U.K. subscribers can recall or even hum it. Now take into account all the ringing overheard on the crowded streets, in buses, and on TV, and well, it's enough, I'd say, to drive a person—or rather, 80 million Nokia users—mad.

When Nokia phones first hit the market, the company's default tune became instantly popular, largely because it was the first melody people recognized when they were starting to buy mobile phones (in case you are wondering, the simple ditty is based on *Gran Vals,* composed by Francisco Terrega in the nineteenth century). Since then, the tone has taken on an almost viral quality. In fact, if you go onto YouTube, you can observe complete strangers playing the Nokia melody on the piano, the guitar, or on a clavier. If you're into hip-hop, there's even a gangsta' Nokia remix. One Web site claims that the impact of the Nokia melody is so great that there've been reports of songbirds chirping it over the skies of London.[13]

All this exposure, one would think, could only spell good news for the brand. But I wasn't so sure. I'd begun to notice that when my Nokia phone rang during the day (when I've forgotten to shut it off), I'd get an uncomfortable *yikes* feeling. My nerves would go on edge. I knew I wasn't alone in feeling this way. Even though the Nokia tune is one of the most successfully branded tunes of our time, something told me there was something off-key going on.

I decided to use the brain-scan study to find out what. So Dr. Calvert and I set out to determine whether a signature sound—like the Nokia ring—makes a brand more or less attractive. The latter scenario of this question intrigued me, too. Are there occasions when a sound can completely derail how buyers perceive a brand? As it turned out, the results of this second study on the power of the senses were even more shocking than the first.

We conducted our study across four different product categories: phones, software, airlines, and various images of London. Then we chose, for each category, associated sounds: the Nokia mobile phone ring, British Airways's "Flower Duet" (which is lifted from Leo Delibes's opera *Lakmé*), Microsoft's start-up and sign-off signature sound; as well as William Blake's lordly hymn, *Jerusalem* (with its lyrics about walking "upon England's mountain green"). Then we showed our volunteers ten separate images per brand, ranging from a British airways jet idling on a tarmac to a computer with Windows's signature colored banners, to a Nokia mobile phone. As a

benchmark, we also showed them images unrelated to the signature sounds.

Next, it was time to roll out the tunes. For our generic,
benchmark brands, we serenaded our volunteers with melo-
dies ranging from random ring tones to an extract from Bach's
Double Violin Concerto.

Dr. Calvert and I once again took seats in the crowded control room as the study got under way. First, we presented individual brands in separate, ten-minute-long segments, or
"runs," during which subjects were first presented with the
sounds alone, followed by the pictures alone, followed by the
images and the sounds simultaneously. Dr. Calvert repeated
this sequence five times in a row—asking participants to signal their preferences for the images, sounds, or image–sound
combinations (again on a scale of one to nine) using their button boxes as we scanned their brains to test their levels of
emotional engagement and their memory encoding for what
they had seen and heard.

Our results revealed that, just as with the image–smell
combinations in the first experiment, when sounds and images were presented simultaneously, they were perceived more
favorably—and left more of an impression—than that sound
or image when presented alone. In most cases, when our volunteers viewed the images and heard the tunes—then viewed
and heard them together—Dr. Calvert and I witnessed activity in the regions of their brains that signaled they were a) paying close attention; b) liked what they saw and heard; c) found
the combination pleasant; and d) would recall the brand, and
probably over the long haul, too.

Thus, Dr. Calvert was able to conclude that consumers' attention is increased when they hear a signature tune while see-

ing a highly recognizable image or logo and, what's more, consumers better recall what they're seeing and hearing when the tune and logo are simultaneous than when their eyes and ears are working alone. In other words, when a branded theme tune and a well-known logo are paired together, we both prefer the brand *and* remember it better.

At least this was the case for most of our image–sound combinations, the London images and *Jerusalem,* as well as the British Airways images and the "Flower Duet." (As for Microsoft, our volunteers found the sight of the brand less positive than its signature sound, but when we presented the Microsoft logo and the Microsoft melody jointly to our subjects, preferences did go up slightly.)

In sum, the fMRI results revealed that three out of four of our brands did well when sound and vision were combined in a congruent way. Our volunteers were emotionally engaged, and there was also evidence of long-term memory encoding. One brand, however, fell catastrophically short.

Nokia. The most familiar, ubiquitous ring tone on Planet Earth had flunked the sound test. Sure, our subjects rated the images of Nokia phones favorably—and why not; they're great phones—but the fMRI results showed that there was an across-the-board, negative emotive response to Nokia's famous ring. So much so, in fact, that just hearing the sound actually suppressed the generally enthusiastic feelings our volunteers' brains showed for the sight of Nokia's phones alone. And the subjects' own ratings further confirmed this result— after hearing the ring, subjects indicated a greater preference for the unrelated benchmark images than for the images of the Nokia phones.

In short, Nokia's ring tone was killing the brand.

But why? To shed further light on this question, Dr. Calvert peered inside our subjects' ventrolateral prefrontal cortices—part of the brain's circuits that processes information about emotion. And intriguingly, what she found was that the sound of the Nokia phone transformed the sight of the phone into a negative somatic marker—in other words, the ring evoked powerful negative associations that completely turned the subjects off from the brand.

This finding stayed with me for a long time. I puzzled over it. The problem with Nokia's ring tone, I realized, was that people had grown to fear, resent, and even hate it. Their brains connected that overfamiliar sound with intrusion, disruption, and feelings of annoyance. They connected it not with the lovelorn vagaries of *Love Actually* but with a romantic dinner or tropical vacation shattered by a phone call from a boss or a movie or a yoga class ruined by the ill-timed ring of an unsilenced phone. In short, for many, Nokia's default ring tone had come to hold all the lyrical charm of a nervous breakdown.

So how do you tell one of the most successful cell phone manufacturers in the world that their pride and glory was dampening, if not outright sinking, the popularity of its brand?[14] It felt a bit like informing John Lennon that the Beatles were fantastic, but Paul had to go. Nokia officials were genuinely shocked when I told them—but after their surprise had worn off, they accepted the findings of our fMRI experiment with aplomb. Time will tell if they do anything with our results.

So what is the future of sensory branding? Pretend it's the year 2030. We're at the same crossroads of the world, Times Square. But instead of billboards and flashing letters, we crane our necks only to see . . . nothing. No twenty-foot-high models. No flashing neon. At the same time, the sidewalk is awash with smells and sounds. A whiff of lemon from a store selling a new, must-have sneaker. A burst of fresh orange from a sporting goods emporium. A clingy perfume wafting from the doors of a just-opened hotel. Is that Vivaldi we're hearing? Sonic Youth? Gregorian chant?

What I'm describing is a subtle sensory assault that doesn't rely exclusively on vision but which summons our nostrils, our eardrums, and our fingertips. Thanks to fMRI, we now know the extent to which the senses are intertwined; that fragrance can make us see, sound can make us smack our lips, and sight can help us imagine sound, taste, and touch—that is, if it's the right pairing of sensory input. For many advertisers, this finding will be a revelation; for consumers, it will validate a strange blurring of the senses that we've always known was there but haven't been able to identify before. Tomorrow's retail world? It will have the distinct smell of cantaloupe, lemongrass, tangerine. It won't be black and white, but in vivid color. It will chirp, waltz, holler, infuse you, and leave you humming. And this assault on your senses will be more effective in winning your mind, your loyalty, and your dollars than you ever thought possible.

Take Alli, GlaxoSmithKline's over-the-counter weight loss treatment. Not only are its colors eye-catchingly vivid (red, blue, yellow and green against a white background), but the uniquely shaped, conveniently portable pill carrier, known as a shuttle, has a gentle, bubbled texture—all of which serves to evoke associations of collaboration and partnership of you and the product embarking on a journey together, hand in hand. Remember, the road to emotion runs through our sensory experiences, and as we've shown in this chapter, emotion is one of the most powerful forces in driving what we buy.

SO FAR, WE have seen many ways in which neuromarketing can shed light on what and why we buy. But can it go so far as to predict the future success or failure of a product? Our next brain-scanning experiment tested the predictive powers of neuromarketing, using the pilot of a TV game show that hundreds of study subjects claimed to hate—but secretly kind of loved.

9

AND THE
ANSWER IS . . .

Neuromarketing and
Predicting the Future

IT WAS, ACCORDING TO its prerelease buzz, a slam dunk, one of those once-in-a-lifetime, can't-miss inventions. Web sites offered tantalizing rumors, wild guesses, and endless *What-if*s. It would revolutionize transportation. It would render cars obsolete. It would banish bicycles and motorcycles from streets and sidewalks. Apple CEO Steve Jobs went so far as to assert that future cities would be built around it. Venture capitalist John Doerr predicted $1 billion in sales for what he foresaw as potentially the most successful product launch in history. In preparation for the anticipated demand of this *thing* (it didn't have a name yet), a New England factory readied itself to assemble roughly 40,000 units a month.

In early December 2001, the Segway PT (short for personal transporter) was released. You remember it, it looked like a rolling upright lawnmower with oversized wheels and a small platform to stand on, something you might motor along in if you were a bionic clone living in the year 2375. When the first three Segways were auctioned off, consumers bought them for more than $100,000 apiece.

But despite all the hype, less than two years later, only six thousand Segways had been sold. And when in 2006 Segway released a new Gen II PT, sales were even more dismal. Despite the novelty of the contraption, at five or six thousand dollars apiece (depending on the model), few people, it seemed, actually wanted to own one. It had been predicted to be one of the most successful, revolutionary products in history, but any way you look at it, the Segway turned out to be a disappointment. It's hardly alone.

As I mentioned in Chapter 1, 80 percent of all product launches fail in the first three months. From soft drinks to paper towels to chocolate bars to hair dryers, the list of fallen products is like a roll call of the dearly departed.

In the U.K., there was a similar version of the Segway story. Was the Sinclair CS, a snow-white, battery-powered, one-seater mini-motorcycle that looked like what Kato rode in beside the Green Hornet, the future of transportation across the British Isles? Well, priced at roughly four hundred pounds sterling, the Sinclair achieved speeds no higher than 15 mph (though you needed to pedal it if you were making your way uphill), effectively permitted fourteen-year-old kids to drive without a license, and after several months (and a whole lot of ridicule) was discontinued, having managed to sell only seventeen thousand units.[1]

Even Coca-Cola has had some embarrassing product flops. Remember 1985's New Coke? Though it fared well in consumer research, once it hit the stores with great fanfare it tanked big-time, and the company was forced to withdraw it. Case closed? No. In 2006, the company announced that it was launching a new line of its famous soft drink containing small amounts of coffee called Coca-Cola BlaK. Two years in development, the product was lauded by Coke executives as "the refreshing taste of an ice-cold Coca-Cola that finishes with a rich essence of coffee." "Only Coca-Cola can deliver that distinct combination of flavors,"[2] Katie Bayne, senior vice-president with Coca-Cola North America, was quoted as saying. But consumers were indifferent, sales were abysmal, and a year or so later, Coke discontinued the product. It was much like when fifteen years earlier, after two years of disappointing sales, the Adolph Coors company quit manufacturing its "beer-branded mineral water," Coors Rocky Mountain Sparkling Water,[3] or when Crystal Pepsi hit the dust in 1993, after only a year on the supermarket shelves.

Certain tobacco products have met similar fates. In 1998, R.J. Reynolds invested approximately $325 million to create a smokeless tobacco known as "Premier." Unfortunately, consumers weren't all that wild about the taste, and the product didn't take. *Reporter* magazine was later quoted as saying, "Inhaling the Premier required vacuum-powered lungs, lighting it virtually required a blowtorch, and, if successfully lit with a match, the sulphur reaction produced a smell and a flavor that left users retching."[4]

And *E.T.: The Extra-Terrestrial* may have been one of the biggest-grossing movies of all time, but its success sure didn't carry over to the E.T. video game for Atari 2600. According to one Web site, "E.T. is notorious for being what many believe to be the worst game ever." As the rumor goes, to get rid of all the unsold copies, the president of Atari had to have them buried in a New Mexico dump.[5]

The point is, whether it's soda or cigarettes or video

games—or any other item under the sun—companies are woefully bad at predicting how we as consumers will respond to their products. As I've been saying throughout this book, because how we *say* we feel about a product can never truly predict how we behave, market research is largely unreliable and can at times seriously mislead a company or even completely undo a product. For example, the Ford Motor Company once asked consumers what features they most wanted in their automobiles. Consumers responded, the supposedly ideal "American Car" model was built—and it flopped.[6]

So is neuromarketing the answer to companies' prayers? Could this nascent yet budding science be the holy grail—what advertisers and marketers and executives have been waiting for all their lives? Better yet, can neuromarketing help companies create products that we consumers actually *like*? And if so, can neuromarketing succeed where market research has resoundingly failed: Can it reliably, scientifically predict the failure of a brand or product?

It was time to find out by screening one of the screechiest TV game shows I'd ever seen in my life. Take a seat—it's time for *Quizmania.*

COULD TV VIEWERS guess the name of the male singer?

It could have been just about anybody. The singer's identity was concealed behind a blue banner in the middle of *Quizmania*'s hallucinogenic set, which included a jukebox, a surfboard, a clump of artificial palm trees, a gumball machine, a caged parrot, and a fleet of giant plastic ice cream cones. Amid the occasional random siren, drum solo, or racetrack fanfare puncturing viewers' ears from offstage, on the bottom of the screen, one by one, letters of a name flipped over, as TV viewers from all over the U.K. were invited to call in and for seventy-five pence (US $1.50) guess who was behind the banner. *Quizmania,* it seemed obvious to me, was *Name That Tune* meets Hangman on amphetamines. And no one seemed more charged-up than the blond female hostess. If callers got the answer wrong, she would slap down her oversized robin's-egg-blue telephone without so much as a "Nice Try."

Hello, Maureen. No, sorry, my love, it's not Tom Jones. Slap.

We have only fifty seconds left! No, love, it's not Elton John. Slap.

Hello, Nathan! Sorry, it's not Cliff Richard! Slap. *People—think of a very famous male singer! For 10,000 pounds! He could be British! He could be American!* Slap. Slap. Slap. Slap.

It was mid-December, 2006, and I was sitting inside a pitch-black room, watching a TV game show pilot produced by the media giant FremantleMedia—the same company that also owns *American Idol.* Described on its Web site as "the U.K.'s most entertaining quiz show," *Quizmania* hadn't debuted yet in the United States, and there was no guarantee it ever would. That was where I came in—to find out if audience members' brains could reliably predict whether or not a new and as-yet-unseen TV program would be a hit with American viewers or a total disaster.

An hour earlier, our subjects, four groups of fifty men and women carefully selected to represent the average demographic of the study, filed into the studio. Following a brief question-and-answer session with one of our team members, volunteers were fitted with their SST caps, the electrodes positioned over specific portions of their brains.

The lights went out and *Quizmania* got under way.

Quizmania wasn't the only TV show that our two hundred volunteers would be watching and testing that afternoon. To ensure an accurate result, we needed additional benchmarks, or measuring sticks, to validate our results, and these we found in the form of two other TV shows, one a "proven failure" and the other a "proven success." Half of our volunteers would be watching the failure, a makeover reality show known as *The Swan.* In it, two perfectly ordinary-looking women are dubbed ugly ducklings, then transformed, through plastic surgery, diet, exercise, tooth-capping, makeup, hair styling, and haute-couture upgrades into, well, swans. At which point, the viewing audience calls in and votes their favorite contestant through to the next round.

The other one hundred subjects would watch, in addition to *Quizmania,* a popular, highly rated TV show called *How Clean Is Your House?* In this half-hour-long British-made reality show, two exacting, middle-aged scolds show up at the door of an unkempt house or apartment, express outrage at its condition, and then make it over into a dream house. For whatever reason, *How Clean Is Your House?* had caught on strongly with TV viewers, while *The Swan* had not.

Massive cash! yelled the manic blond hostess, as *Quizmania* surged forward. *Life-changing cash! Callers, we're now playing for 60,000 pounds!* she bawled, until one caller finally got it right. (Iggy Pop for those who are curious.)

Twenty-four hours earlier, we'd given each viewer a DVD of the programs in question, asked them to watch both shows, then sleep on it, in order to minimize the "novelty" effect many of us experience when we're watching something for the first time. Now, as the room went dark, Professor Silberstein and his colleagues kept watch on a series of large computer screens in an adjacent lab. Our volunteers would have two opportunities to express what was on their minds. First, each one would fill out a questionnaire asking them how they felt about the shows they had just seen. The next step would be to peer inside their brains. When the study was over, the researchers would check the results of the SST studies against the questionnaires to find out if they matched up.

HENLIKE AND ACID-TONGUED, Kim and Aggie, a pair of middle-aged British busybodies and self-described Cleaning Queens, entered the row house in a New York City borough. Their expressions were eloquent. "We are totally and utterly disgusted," one of them remarked, eyeing the squalor before them.

Janet and Kathy, college-aged sisters, lived alone. Earlier, they'd announced that their vocations in life were "clubbing" and "shopping." Like, no kidding. Clothing and shoes were strewn everywhere, from the living room to the bedroom. You could barely make out the vague outlines of furniture. The kitchen with its rancid refrigerator and grease-clogged stovetop burners was hardly an improvement. In the bathroom, the ceiling above the shower was peeling and streaked with so much black-purple mold it looked like a starless winter sky. One of the Cleaning Queens even began to itch.

"But we don't *know* how to clean," one of the sisters whined.

Two smart, grossed-out Brits versus two pampered, slovenly sisters. Amid somewhat scripted-sounding sisterly bickering ("That's *her* stuff!" "No, it's *her* stuff!"), out came the industrial-sized garbage bags and Swiffer cleaning cloths and in came a team of professional air consultants, who, after finding that colonies of aspergillus and penicillium molds had made the bathroom ceiling their home, recommended the entire shower stall be retiled.

Soon, a sisterly pigsty had been transformed into a palace—Zenlike in appearance, dotted here and there with flickering white pillar candles. Makeover complete. Followed by hugs, disbelief, and lots of *OhmyGod! OhmyGodthankyousososomuch!*

Our question: Would viewers prefer this show over *Quizmania*? And how would it fare against *The Swan*?

Professor Silberstein called a week later with the results.

"PLEASE TICK THE box that best describes how you feel about the program you saw."

I would never miss an episode.

I would watch it in preference to other programs if
   I'm at home.

I would watch it if there was nothing better on.

I would watch it only if I was with my partner or a
   friend who wanted to watch it.

I would never watch it.

This was the questionnaire that our two hundred respondents were handed following our study. First, we asked this question about our two benchmark test shows, *The Swan* and *How Clean Is Your House?* As I suspected, the pencil-and-paper responses didn't quite reflect the success or failure status of each show that we knew to be true—more evidence that how we say we feel about something and how we actually behave rarely match up. In fact, despite the fact that *How Clean Is Your House?* had been a huge hit and *The Swan* a flop, they were just about neck and neck in terms of how likely our volunteers *claimed* they would be to watch. Yet their SST results said otherwise; the results showed that our subjects were far more emotionally engaged when watching *How Clean Is Your House?* than when watching *The Swan;* in other words, their brains' responses were consistent with how those two shows had actually done, even though their questionnaire responses were not.

So what was the verdict on *Quizmania?* On their questionnaires, viewers rated Fremantle's pilot program as the one they were *least* likely to watch—far less likely than the other two programs. Based on their written responses, it seemed our study subjects hated *Quizmania.* Loathed it even. The pencil-and-paper results were almost unanimous. Our viewers said they would rather watch anything *but.*

Next, we looked at the SST results. And the brains of these same two hundred men and women told a different story entirely. While watching *How Clean Is Your House?* viewer engagement (measured in the frontal part of the brain) was shown to be "consistently high," while viewer engagement while watching *The Swan* was deemed "low to moderate." No surprises there. The subjects' brains had merely confirmed what we already knew: *How Clean Is Your House?* was a proven ratings winner, while *The Swan,* as I knew, was not.

But when it came to *Quizmania,* despite their unanimously unfavorable responses, our subjects' brains, all two hundred of them, had *liked* it. They might have said they hated the phony palm trees, the giant ice cream cones, the manic host-ess, and the Hangman-on-speed premise, but their brains in-dicated otherwise.

The SST scans showed that although our subjects rated the unaired pilot program *Quizmania* as the show they were *least* likely to watch, viewers' brains were actually *more* engaged when watching *Quizmania* than when watching *The Swan,* a show they had claimed to have liked, proving to me, once again, that what people say and how they really feel are often polar opposites.

In short, based on viewers' brains' responses to the three programs we tested that day in Los Angeles, *The Swan* was the least engaging, *How Clean Is Your House?* the most engaging, and *Quizmania* lay somewhere in between the two. Therefore, we concluded (with a 99 percent degree of statistical certainty) that *Quizmania*—if and when it ever aired—would be more successful than *The Swan,* but less successful than *How Clean Is Your House?*

And indeed, in the U.K. it was. In other words, the brain scans accurately predicted the show's U.K. performance. And while the program now airs in Australia, Brazil, and a long list of other countries, FremantleMedia is holding off on airing the program in the United States. Based on the results of test runs, they are convinced that the show would, indeed, per-form just as our brain scans predicted. But is it worth it?

Which leads me to wonder: What might have happened if neuromarketing had been around a decade or two ago? Would New Coke have ever appeared on a supermarket shelf? Would Premium smokeless tobacco have made it out of the lab? Would a single Segway or Sinclair have rolled past our windows?

I believe the answer is no. Instead, the companies would have been able to foresee that these products would fail, would have halted production, and saved hundreds of millions of dollars in the process. Which then begs the question, now that companies do have this powerful tool at their fingertips, how will they use it? I predict that soon, more and more companies (at least those who can afford it) will be trading in their pencils for SST caps. That traditional market research—questionnaires, surveys, focus groups, and so on—will gradually take on a smaller and smaller role, and neuromarketing will become the primary tool companies use to predict the success or failure of their products. And what's more, I predict that as neuromarketing becomes more popular and more in demand, it will become cheaper, easier, and more available to companies than ever before. And in turn, it will become even more popular and more widespread.

ARE YOU AT all interested in sex? That got your attention, didn't it? We're about to take a look at whether sex in advertising works in seducing our interest in a product or whether it in fact backfires. From Calvin Klein to an Italian ad campaign that will make you (I hope) shudder, we're about to put an age-old question to the test: Does sex sell?

10

LET'S SPEND THE
NIGHT TOGETHER

Sex in Advertising

A YOUNG WOMAN SPRAWLS across the hood of the new 1966 Ford Mustang. Surrounding her, delicate flower petals spell out the number six (in reference to both the year and the car's six-cylinder engine). The tagline underneath? *Six and the Single Girl.*

A National Airlines stewardess makes come-hither eyes at readers from the pages of a glossy magazine, circa 1971. "I'm Cheryl," reads the tagline. "Fly me." A year later, a 23 percent increase in passengers prompts National Airlines to release a series of follow-up ads in which a pack of beautiful stewardesses vows, "I'm going to fly you like you've never been flown before."

The year is 1977. A seductive Scandinavian blonde bites down suggestively on a pearl necklace before purring, "For men, nothing takes it off like Noxzema medicated shave." As the man in her life vigorously shaves his beard, the blonde adds, "Take it off. Take it *all* off."

Decades ago, these ads scandalized many Americans.

What's happening to our culture, people wondered? Is advertising going too far? Are we being corrupted by sex?

But the television and print ads from the sixties and seventies were tame when stacked up against those of today. After all, bear in mind that the female perched atop the Mustang, the Noxzema model, and the airline stewardesses were all fully clothed—even the man shaving was wearing an undershirt. Compare this to the nearly naked bodies that sell us everything from perfume to alcohol to underwear nowadays. Take an ad I saw recently, for example, which featured a nearly naked man with his hands cuffed behind him and his mouth gagged, while a long, limber, luscious pair of shapely legs belonging to a dominatrix appeared behind tempting him with her . . . German vacuum cleaner. Or the ad featuring another nearly naked man, his briefs tumbling over his loins, a woman behind him caressing his chest in an ad for, of all things, Renova toilet paper. Or the one showing a silhouette of a Volvo's driver's seat with its parking break extending in the air—precisely like an erect penis—over the tagline, "We're just as excited as you are."[1]

In 2007, the ads for designer Tom Ford's new fragrance featured a naked woman clutching the bottle either against her thoroughly Brazilian-waxed, slightly spread legs or between her bare breasts. The same year, a German company known as Vivaeros claiming to have bottled the smell of sex in the form of a "beguiling vaginal scent" released a new perfume called Vulva (I'll leave the design of the logo to your imagination) and began selling it as a fragrance for men.[2]

Or consider the ads for two new fragrances recently created by the rap mogul P. Diddy and singer Mariah Carey. P. Diddy's cologne, known as Unforgivable Woman, was released in the U.K. with an accompanying promotional film featuring a fully dressed Combs and a nearly naked super-model engaging in, shall we say, intimate behavior (the ad was rejected in the United States because of its suggestive content). Mariah Carey took a more sensual approach: the thirty-second ads for M feature a naked Mariah crooning and caressing herself in the cascading dew of a rain forest.[3]

According to a 2005 book entitled *Sex in Advertising: Perspectives on the Erotic Appeal,* roughly one-fifth of all advertising today uses overt sexual content to sell its products.[4] If you need evidence, just browse through the latest issue of *Vogue,* pay a visit to your nearest American Apparel store, or gape at the latest twenty-foot Calvin Klein billboards overlooking Times Square.

Or drop by Abercrombie & Fitch. When I visit the chain's stores, inevitably, my eyes are drawn to the mannequins in the front windows. It's hard *not* to look—the females are all designed with unnaturally large breasts and the male mannequins with an abnormally pronounced endowment. And if men's jeans or women's blouses are on display, usually there's a deliberately placed rip affording a peekaboo glimpse of checkered boxer shorts here, a lacy bra strap there.

But it's not just clothing and perfume companies using the overt suggestion of sex to peddle their products. One billboard promoting Las Vegas's Hard Rock Casino features a pair of bikini bottoms lowered around a woman's calves. The tagline: *Get ready to buck all night.*[5] And what about a commercial for the Nikon Coolpix camera featuring a naked Kate Moss with the tagline *See Kate Like You've Never Seen Her Before.* Even family-style restaurants aren't exempt. In a witty but salacious takeoff on nonsmoking patch commercials,

Nando's, an Australian chain of poultry restaurants, show-cases a naked, pole-dancing mother who's fighting her chicken "pangs" but, unable to place a patch on her bare, wriggling bottom, has to resort to Nando's poultry chewing gum.

And let's not forget Virgin Atlantic's edgy ad campaigns. Since 2000, British Airways—Virgin's archrival—has sponsored the London Eye, the giant Ferris wheel and observation booth that sits on the banks of the Thames. Yet when the London Eye found itself experiencing construction problems that delayed its opening by over a year, Virgin founder Richard Branson spied his chance. He hired a dirigible to fly over the oversized Ferris wheel with a message reading *"British Airways can't get it up."* (No lawsuit ensued, because no Virgin logo appeared; yet consumers immediately recognized the rival airline's tone of voice.) Virgin's ad for its in-flight entertainment system? *Nine inches of pure pleasure.*

In short, sex in advertising is everywhere—not just in TV commercials, magazines, retail spaces, and on the Internet, but on the side of the bus you take to work, in the aisles of your local deli, even in the airspace above your head. But does sex necessarily sell? How effective are scantily clad models, sexually suggestive packaging, or heart-stoppingly attractive product spokespeople in actually seducing us to buy certain products over others?

In a 2007 experiment, Ellie Parker and Adrian Furnham of University College London set out to study how well we recall sexually suggestive commercials. They divided sixty young adults into four groups. Two groups watched an episode of *Sex and the City* during which the female characters discuss whether or not they're good in bed, while the other two watched an episode of the decidedly unerotic family sitcom

Malcolm in the Middle. During the commercial breaks, one segment of each group viewed a series of sexually suggestive ads
for products like shampoo, beer, and perfume, while the other
two groups watched ads with no sexual content whatsoever.
The question, once the study was over: What do you remember? Turns out that the subjects who had been shown the sexually suggestive advertisements were no better able to recall
the names of the brands and products they had seen than the
subjects who had viewed the unerotic ads.

What's more, the group that watched *Sex and the City* actually had *worse* recall of the advertisements they had seen than
the *Malcolm in the Middle* viewers—it seemed their memory of
the sexually explicit commercials had been eclipsed by the sexual content in the show itself. It would appear, the researchers
concluded, "that sex does not sell anything other than itself."[6]

Further research by a New England–based company called
MediaAnalyzer Software & Research found that in some
cases, sexual stimuli actually interfere with the effectiveness of
an ad. They showed four hundred subjects print ads ranging
in suggestiveness from racy cigarette ads to bland credit card
entreaties, then instructed the subjects to use their computer
mouses to indicate where exactly on the page their gaze in-
stinctively migrated. Unsurprisingly, the men spent an inordi-
nate amount of time passing their mouses over the women's
breasts. But in doing so, they largely bypassed the brand name,
logo, and other text. In other words, the sexually suggestive
material blinded them to all the other information in the ad—
even the name of the product itself.

In fact, as it turned out, only 9.8 percent of the men who
had viewed the ads with the sexual content were able to remember the correct brand or product in question, compared

to almost 20 percent of the men who had seen the nonsexual ones. And this effect was replicated in the women—only 10.85 percent remembered the correct brand or product featured in the sexual ads, whereas 22.3 percent recalled the brand or product in the ones with the neutral content. The research team dubbed this phenomenon the Vampire Effect, referring to the fact that the titillating content was sucking attention from what the ad was actually trying to say.

THOUGH SEX IN advertising has been around for close to a century—a 1920s print ad shows a nearly naked woman hawking Shrader Universal valve caps, tire pressure gauges, and dust caps—when American consumers think of the birth of sex and advertising, a single name often comes to mind: Calvin Klein. Ever since 1980, when a fifteen-year-old Brooke Shields told the world, "Nothing comes between me and my Calvins," the designer has become renowned for his mastery of the art of sexually suggestive advertising. But those 1980 Brooke Shields ads, whose implicit waft of adolescent sex drove up jeans sales to approximately two million pairs a month, were just the beginning of a marketing strategy that made sexual allure synonymous with the Calvin Klein brand. Mopey shirtless grunge couples. Doe-eyed models. A sinewy teenager in crotch-hugging blue boxer shorts poised over a pubescent girl in an obvious prelude to sex. Over the next few years, Klein's billboards of young, chiseled males and slender, busty female underwear models created a huge media sensation, making stars out of the likes of Mark Wahlberg, Antonio Sabato Jr., Christy Turlington, and Kate Moss—all players in a global empire that, by 1984, was worth nearly a billion dollars a year.[7]

Naturally, these provocative ads sparked public outrage—not to mention stories in *Time, Newsweek,* and *People,* among other magazines. CBS and NBC dropped some of the Shields commercials in protest. Women against Pornography opposed the ads. Gloria Steinem called them worse than violent pornography, but even this didn't come between consumers and their Calvins. In fact, it helped sales, and soon Klein controlled nearly 70 percent of the jeans market at major retailers like Bloomingdale's. "Did we sell more jeans?" Klein was quoted as saying. "Yes, of course! It was great."[8]

In 1995, Klein upped the ante. He released a series of provocative TV commercials whose unsteady camera work, low lighting, grainy resolution, and setting in what resembled a cheap, wood-paneled San Fernando Valley motel room appeared to deliberately mimic low-budget 1970s porn videos. In them, a throaty, off-camera male voice asked the pubescent models suggestive questions such as, *Do you like your body? Have you ever made love before a camera?*

The American public was indeed aroused. The American Family Association rolled out a well-orchestrated letter campaign to retailers, urging them not to carry the Calvin Klein brand in their stores. Soon, the U.S. Department of Justice even launched an investigation into whether Klein had violated child pornography laws (turns out he hadn't, and was never charged). In response to the outcry, Klein denied all accusations of pornography, claiming they merely depicted "glamour . . . an inner quality that can be found in regular people in the most ordinary setting."[9]

In the end, Klein pulled the ads, but the controversy created news—and more free publicity—in itself. And his new line of jeans, specifically tailored so the groin and the buttocks seam are both raised to emphasize the crotch and the rear end, became among the most coveted pieces of clothing of the year.

The designer kept pushing the envelope. It was working, wasn't it? In 1999, Klein ran full-page ads in several periodicals (including the *New York Times Magazine*) that featured two boys no older than five or six jumping around on a couch wearing nothing but Calvin Klein underwear. Naturally, this created a fresh new wave of outrage among antipornography groups, child's rights advocates, and the general public. Though a company spokesperson claimed that the ads were intended to "capture the same warmth and spontaneity that you find in a family snapshot," a day later Klein very publicly scrapped the entire campaign, including a large billboard of the same boys that was set to debut in Times Square.[10]

In the same way that banned books become the must-read phenomena of the year, more than a few observers were by now realizing that Klein's tactic of unveiling sexually suggestive ads, getting consumers in a lather, then abruptly yanking them was in fact a PR maneuver as risqué and attention-grabbing as the ads themselves. Klein's growth was spectacular throughout the seventies and early eighties—his brand was so ubiquitous that blue jeans became known simply as "Calvins."

Since 2002, when, facing competition from heavyweights like The Gap, Klein was forced to sell his business to the apparel giant Phillips Van Heusen, a number of other brands have taken a page from his handbook and capitalized on the fact that controversy—even more than sex—sells, though some have managed this trick more successfully than others. In 2003, for example, Abercrombie & Fitch released an extremely racy, soft-porn, end-of-year catalog that prompted a boycott by the National Coalition for the Protection of Children and Families and a highly unfavorable *60 Minutes* segment. And when a recent Dolce & Gabbana print ad picturing what looked like a gang rape was pulled in response to protests by women in Spain, Italy, and the United States, the brand suffered. Still, while companies may drive customers away in the short term with such suggestive advertising, the fact remains that these ads, offensive though they may be, are that much more memorable for their shock value.[11]

And when it comes to shock value, the new kid on the block is the Los Angeles–based American Apparel. Its racy, slightly seedy advertisements featuring pouty, underaged models (many of whom are company employees) provocatively posed—often with their legs spread, and always in varying states of undress—have achieved their goal: generating controversy. Since 2005, when the company came under attack for degrading women, promoting pornography, and even encouraging rape, it is doing better than ever—with 151 stores in eleven different countries, sales were estimated at approximately $300 million in 2006.

But the question remains: Is it the sex that is selling or the controversy? Evidence points to the latter. Of course, sex, which is innately hardwired to our survival as a species, is powerful in and of itself, yet in many cases it is the attention that can be more effective than the suggestive content itself. And while sex and controversy are, at least in the world of advertising, inextricably linked, when it comes to what truly influences our behavior and gets us to buy, controversy can often be the more potent factor.

IF SEX DOESN'T always sell, what about beauty? Are ads, commercials, or product packages featuring supermodels and preternaturally attractive celebrities actually more effective than those featuring "real" people? Well, evidence suggests that just as sex hijacks our attention away from the crucial information in an advertisement, so, too, can extreme beauty or celebrity. According to an article in *Ad Age* magazine, The Gap's use of famous people, including Lenny Kravitz and Joss Stone, in ads has been a resounding failure.[12]

Think about über-attractive product spokespeople like Nicole Kidman or George Clooney. We remember their pretty faces, but do we really remember the brand of perfume or make of watch they're trying to sell? It's kind of like a few years ago, when the British comedian John Cleese did a series of clever antismoking commercials that failed in the U.K. People loved them because they were so deft and funny, but viewers were so distracted by the humor—and Cleese's strong presence—that the antismoking message took a backseat. Similarly, the English comedian Dawn French's pitch for the Cable Association and the English actor Leonard Rossiter's ads for the Italian vermouth Cinzano were, in my opinion, two more examples of how celebrities can overshadow what an ad is trying to communicate.[13]

A recent study at the University of Florida showed that women, in fact, are often turned off by extremely attractive

Beauty Doesn't always buy because people identify w/ people who look more like us

models. Approximately 250 young women viewed an identical set of fashion magazine photos, which included celebrities such as Uma Thurman and Lindsay Lohan. They were then asked to place the models in six separate categories of beauty: sensual exotic, trendy, cute, girl next door, sex kitten, and classic feminine. But the results showed that the women collapsed those half-a-dozen categories into two much more general categories: sexy and wholesome. The women were next asked for their emotional responses to the images. According to the study, the more provocative and sexual the women rated the model's expression and attire, the more bored or disinterested the women were by the ad. On the other hand, the more wholesome, natural, un-made-up, and clothed the models were, the more positive the women's reactions.[14] This dovetails with a 2001 survey carried out by market research firm Market Facts, which showed that nearly twice as many people were more likely to buy an advertised product if it showed images of "love" (53 percent) than if it showed images that alluded to sex (26 percent).[15]

Another reason beauty doesn't always sell is the simple fact that we as consumers are far more likely to identify with people who look more like us and less like Scarlett Johansson. Think about it. Let's say you're a suburban mom shopping for a new car. You see an ad for an Audi convertible driven by a bright-eyed twenty-something model with smooth skin and perfectly windswept hair. Then you see an ad for a Subaru Outback with an older, less attractive, and slightly disheveled driver (the toll, no doubt, of a demanding schedule of housekeeping, school pickups, cello lessons, and soccer games) at the helm. Which do you choose? Maybe deep down you want the Audi, but in the end, you go for the Subaru because think to yourself, *That woman is more like me.* Even more to the point, *What the heck does a beautiful actress have to do with cars and highways and great gas mileage?*

Consider what's happening in the worlds of television and advertising today. From *The Simple Life* to *The Hills,* reality-based TV dominates network programming. Taking a cue from YouTube, more and more advertisers are beginning to recognize that consumers enjoy watching—and empathizing with—people like themselves.

This may help explain why one of the hottest trends in commercials today is consumer-generated advertising—advertising that allows everyday people to participate in the campaign. Because ads and commercials created by everyday consumers tend not to feature models, but rather average-looking people who resemble ourselves, we can connect and identify with them more easily. Moreover, average-looking people seem more inviting, as though welcoming us to the brand.

Take Axe deodorant, the leader in its category. Recently the company challenged consumers to come up with "The World's Dirtiest Film," inviting the public to send in their muddiest, filthiest ads. One of the most popular (which has naturally migrated over to YouTube) featured hundreds of women dressed in skimpy bikinis involved in a kind of Iron-Woman competition. But were these women models or even unknown beauties? No. Many of them were attractive, but not in a supermodel kind of way.

Many companies are acknowledging that life has become, for many, the ultimate reality show. Heinz, too, recently jumped on the user-generated advertising bandwagon and created a "Top This! TV Challenge" inviting fans to upload their amateur ketchup commercials onto a Web site and vote for their favorites. Similarly, KFC recently ran a commercial made up of snippets from its fans' homemade Web videos, showing everyday, average-looking consumers' exuberant, if slightly exaggerated, reaction to the company's new menu of trans-fat–free chicken.

So why do we often respond more favorably to "real" or "ordinary" people in print and TV ads? In large part, it's tied to our desire for authenticity. By their sheer ordinariness, real people suggest an authentic backstory. And because they don't look like models, we feel like they really believe in what they are selling. Yet when we see supermodels, no matter how glamorous and seductive they may be to the human eye, we intrinsically feel that whatever they claim about the product is phony. They're not telling a story; they're acting in one.

If you need more evidence that unglamorous people can sell products, consider that Mikhail Gorbachev, hardly anyone's idea of a glamour-puss, shows up in the latest Louis Vuitton commercial—and also appears in a Russian Pizza Hut ad along with his granddaughter.[16]

Indeed, what we're beginning to witness in the advertising world today is a fascinating marriage between the world of the airbrushed supermodel and the world of the ordinary consumer—a blurry union between perfect and not so perfect. And in our increasingly user-generated world, as our desire for authenticity grows, I suspect marketers will be selling by using more and more charismatic yet ordinary people with real stories. Dove's highly successful "real beauty" campaign, which featured stories from real women of all shapes and sizes, and a recent campaign rolled out by a French company called Comptoir des Cotonniers, in which clothing lines are modeled by "real-life" mothers and daughters, are good examples.

THE QUESTION REMAINS: If sex and beauty don't necessarily sell products, why are they so prevalent in marketing and advertising? Thanks to our brain-scan experiments, for the first time ever, we know the brain science behind why. And the answer lies in the mirror neuron.

In an earlier chapter, we saw how, when we see attractive, scantily clad young people, our mirror neurons allow us to imagine ourselves as being equally cool, attractive, and desirable. The same goes for sex appeal. By simply observing a gorgeous model adorned in a pair of lacy underwear in a Victoria's Secret catalog, most women can imagine the feel and touch of it against their own skin—and feel equally sexy and seductive as the woman in the ad. As I mentioned earlier, this phenomenon is what underlies most advertising nowadays, whether it's a perfume commercial with Scarlett Johansson or a diamond ad with Elizabeth Taylor.

Or if you're a man, chances are that you've come across the explicit photographs of male crotches on the labels of underwear boxes. Doesn't matter if you're buying boxer briefs, tighty-whiteys, or jockstrap-like thongs, there are bulges everywhere. These may *appear* to be targeted at gay men, but in fact they are less about sexual attraction than about visions of one's ideal self. Thanks to mirror neurons, just looking at those idealized bodies lets all those average guys out there feel as confident and sexy as though those bodies were theirs. Now, enter girlfriends and wives. Who do you think is buying most men their underwear? You guessed it. In fact, I would estimate that more than three-quarters of all pairs of male underwear are bought by women for men—a phenomenon known as the Gillette Strategy (referring to the widespread assumption that 90 percent of all Gillette shavers are bought by women for the men in their lives). After all, women, too, are happy to picture their man looking as fit, virile, and strapping as those models in their underwear.

Unfortunately, sometimes the intended effects of mirror neurons can backfire. Consider a recent public service campaign in Milan, courtesy of the Italian fashion label Nolita, aimed at discouraging anorexia among young fashion models. Nolita, which is based in northeast Italy, targets young women with midrange apparel and has a long history of running edgy ad campaigns. Yet the brand has never attracted major attention in fashion circles—until now.[17]

Nolita's billboard ads feature an emaciated, cadaverous-looking twenty-seven-year-old Frenchwoman named Isabelle Caro who weighs in at all of sixty-eight pounds. Above her head is the tagline *No. Anorexia.* According to one news site, the photographer, Oliviero Toscani, created the images "to show everyone the reality of this illness, caused in most cases by the stereotypes imposed by the world of fashion."[18] Yet it seems to have had an opposite effect. Just as the gruesome health warnings on the cigarette packages made smokers crave cigarettes, these images of the deathly thin model made anorexics want to emulate her, thanks to their brains' mirror neurons whispering to them, "You should look so skinny"—

we'll go back to the same-old, same-old. In other words, as the president of Italy's Association for the Study of Anorexia explained, "far from helping women suffering from anorexia, the photo may make many of them feel envious of the model and determined to become even thinner than her."

This is an unfortunate consequence of a fact that I continuously remind myself: that sex in advertising is all about wish fulfillment, about planting dreams inside consumers' brains. Which is why I believe that in the near future sex in advertising is just going to continue to increase across the globe—and that it will only get edgier, more extreme, and more in-your-face. We're going to begin seeing sexual images in ways we've never seen before. And just as we now look back and puzzle over our outrage over the fully clothed Noxzema girl and National Airlines airline hostesses, we'll someday look back at the release of Vulva perfume as almost delightfully quaint.

Why? Because whether it succeeds in getting us to buy or not, sex is perhaps more accessible today than it's ever been. Young consumers no longer have to steal their father's dirty magazine, or sneak into a triple-X-rated movie—now, every kind of sex imaginable is only a mouse click away. And because we're so overexposed to images of sex, in coming years advertisers will be forced to fight for our attention by upping the ante with more and more overt sexuality. We've seen it all and done it all—so the shock effect has faded. But I predict this will ultimately backfire; a decade from now, most of us will have become so desensitized to sex in advertising we won't even notice it anymore.

And advertisers will backtrack—and start all over again.

In other words, eventually I believe sex in advertising will go underground. Sexual ads in the future will get sneakier, subtler. They'll suggest, but they won't complete. They'll flirt, but take it no further than that. They'll propose, then leave the rest up to our imaginations. In short, you could say that the future of sex in ads will be to kick-start a journey into our own heads.

Now it's time to let your brain take over.

11

CONCLUSION

Brand New Day

IN THIS BOOK, YOU'VE witnessed an historic meeting between science and marketing. A union of apparent opposites that, I hope, has shed new light on how you make decisions about what you buy—everything from food, to cell phones, to cigarettes, even to political candidates—and why. Now you and your brain have a better understanding of what is behind this advertising assault that plays on our hidden preferences, unconscious desires, and irrational dreams, and that exerts such an outsized influence on our behavior, each and every day. Thanks to neuroimaging, we can now understand better what *really* drives our behavior, our opinions, our preference for Corona over Budweiser, iPods over Zunes, or McDonald's over Wendy's.

It's bizarre, when you think about it, how long it's taken for science and marketing to come together. After all, science has been around for as long as there've been human beings puzzling over why we behave the way we do. And marketing, a twentieth-century invention, has been asking the same sorts of questions for over a hundred years. Science is hard fact, the final word. Marketers and advertisers, on the other hand, have spent over a century throwing spaghetti at the wall and hoping it will stick.

The fact is that most marketing, advertising, and branding strategies are a guessing game—and those ads that happen to meet success are considered, in hindsight, pure kismet. Until now, marketers and advertisers haven't really known what drives our behavior, so they've had to rely on luck, coincidence, chance, or repeating the same old tricks all over again. But now that we know that roughly 90 percent of our consumer buying behavior is unconscious, the time has come for a paradigm shift. Earlier, I compared advertisers to Christopher Columbus gripping a simple, scribbled map of an earth he believed to be flat. Thanks to brain-scanning experiments, we're now seeing an almost Aristotelian shift in thinking; companies are starting to realize that the world, in fact, is round. No more sailing and tacking and falling off the edge of the world and into the abyss. There is much to be learned from the science of neuromarketing. Let me give you a few examples.

Among the companies taking advantage of neuromarketing is Christian Dior, which put its new fragrance, J'adore, to the fMRI test, assessing everything from its scent to its colors to its ad placements. The company won't say what it uncovered, but it's worth noting that J'adore has been one of the most blazingly successful launches at Christian Dior in years.[1]

To figure out why her CD sales had fallen over the past two years, the management team behind a popular Latin American singer recently hired a well-known consulting company, Mind-Code, which specializes in the indirect signals that ads, brands, and personas send to our mammalian brains. In an effort to conquer the American market, the management team had altered the singer's song lyrics to make them 100 percent English so as better to target U.S. listening tastes. Yet could this possibly be the reason for the unexpected slump in the singer's career? MindCode's careful analysis said it was, and advised the singer's management team to reintroduce Spanish lyrics into her songs (or at least, mix them up judiciously with English lyrics), which she did. A few months later, the singer's CD sales had rebounded spectacularly.

Microsoft and the personal computer are getting into the act, too, finally acknowledging that "human beings are often poor reporters of their own actions," according to a company spokesperson.[2] Which is why the company plans to use EEGs to record the electrical activity in people's brains to see what emotions—from surprise to satisfaction to incredible, hair-pulling frustration (a feeling not unfamiliar to most Microsoft users)—people felt as they interacted with their computers.

Unilever, the international giant that manufactures everything from Pond's Cold Cream to Lipton Tea, recently teamed up with a brain-scanning company to find out how consumers truly felt about its best-selling Eskimo ice cream bars. And what did they discover? It wasn't just that consumers liked their particular brand of ice cream; eating ice cream, it turns out, creates even greater visceral pleasure for us than either chocolate or yogurt.

Neuroscientists have even studied how our brains make decisions about how much we're willing to pay for a product. When subjects view luxury products such as Louis Vuitton and Gucci being sold at full price, both the nucleus accumbens and the anterior cingulate light up, showing the pleasure of anticipatory reward mixed with the conflict about buying such an expensive doodad. But when consumers are shown the same products priced at a significant discount, the "conflict" signal decreases as the reward activation simultaneously goes *up.*

In a related study, researchers from Stanford University and the California Institute of Technology asked twenty volunteers to rank their enjoyment of differently priced wines under an fMRI. The trick: two of the wines were presented twice, one with an expensive price tag, the other normally priced. The findings? When the expensive wine was presented, there was a flurry of activity in subjects' medial orbitofrontal cortices, where they perceive pleasantness—indicating that the higher price of a product enhances our enjoyment of it. As Antonio Rangel, an associate professor of economics at Cal Tech, concluded, "we enjoy our purchases . . . because we paid more."[3]

Yet few neuromarketing studies could be more intriguing than one carried out in early 2007 by a team of researchers at UCLA. Using an fMRI, they scanned the brains of ten people—five men and five women—as they reviewed last year's Super Bowl commercials. A high-stakes experiment to say the least, considering that in 2006 the price for a thirty-second Super Bowl ad reached a new high: $2.4 million for a single spot, the most expensive in TV history.

One ad, created by car giant General Motors, trumpeted the automaker's 100,000-mile warranty. It opens with a shot of a robot working at an automotive assembly line. All is business as usual until the robot fumbles a screw and the assembly line comes to a stop. In short order, the robot is out of a job, homeless, despondent, and reduced to begging on the sidewalks, until finally, he ends his life by hurling himself off a bridge. In the last few seconds, it turns out the robot was having a nightmare, one intended to demonstrate the high-stakes perfectionism of GM workers.

Another ad, debuted by Nationwide Annuities, starred the indomitable Kevin Federline, Britney Spears's ex-husband. Dressed all in white, K-Fed unwinds himself from a red sports car as bikini-wearing females cluster around him. In a reverse twist on the GM ad, the entire scenario is revealed as a workplace reverie. The next shot reveals the real-life Kevin Federline manning the counter of a fast-food chain. The tagline? *Life comes at you fast.* The obvious subtext is that a man can be on top of the world one moment and working a minimum-wage job the next—so he'd be wise to protect himself by investing with Nationwide.

As the volunteers viewed the two commercials, fMRI scans revealed a noticeable amount of stimulation in their amygdalas, the region of the brain that generates dread, anxiety, and the fight-or-flight impulse.

In other words, the commercials had scared viewers, leaving them upset, rattled, anxious, on edge. The subjects might have been thinking about the uncertainty of the economy or their own job security, or they might just have found the robot—or Kevin Federline—inherently fear-inducing. Point is, the brain scans revealed information of incredible value to GM and Nationwide Annuities: that their $2.4 million commercials not only weren't working, they were scaring people away.[4]

But perhaps the biggest lesson companies have learned from neuromarketing is that traditional research methods, like asking consumers why they buy a product, only get at a minuscule part of the brain processes that underlie decision-making. Most of us can't really say, "I bought that Louis Vuitton bag because it appealed to my sense of vanity, and I want my friends to know I can afford a $500 purse, too," or "I bought that Ralph Lauren shirt because I want to be perceived as an easygoing prepster who doesn't have to work, even though all my credit cards are maxed out." As we have seen again and again, most of our buying decisions aren't remotely conscious. Our brain makes the decision and most of the time we aren't even aware of it.

But despite what we are now starting to learn about how our brain influences our buying behavior, there is still much more yet for scientists to discover. So how will the findings of neuroscience affect how (and what) we buy in the near future? I believe that our national obsession with buying and consuming is just going to escalate, as marketers become better and better at targeting our subconscious wishes and desires.

Though in some cases (for example, the Nationwide commercial, which left viewers generally anxious and rattled), fear can drive consumers away from a product, there is no denying that fear exerts an extremely powerful effect on the brain. In fact, when fear-based advertising plays less on our generalized anxieties and more on our insecurities about ourselves, it can be one of the most persuasive—and memorable—types of advertising out there. Given that, I predict we'll be seeing more and more marketing based on fear in the years to come. Remember that the more stress we're under in our world, and the more fearful we are, the more we seek out solid foundations. The more we seek out solid foundations, the more we become dependent on dopamine. And the more dopamine surges through our brains, the more we want, well, *stuff*. It's as though we've climbed aboard a fast-moving escalator and can't get off to save our lives. Perhaps George W. Bush knew a little something about the brain—when asked what Americans could do to contribute in the fearful, unsettled days and weeks after 9/11, he replied with a simple monosyllabic: *"Shop."*

Soon, more and more companies will go out of their way to play on our fears and insecurities about ourselves, to make us think we're not good enough, that if we don't buy their product, we'll somehow be missing out. That we'll become more and more imperfect; that we'll have dandruff or bad skin or dull hair or be overweight or have a lousy fashion sense. That if we don't use this shaving cream, women will walk by us without a glance, that if we don't pop this anti-depressant we'll be a wallflower forever, that if we don't wear this brand of lingerie no man will ever marry us (and need we remind you that you're getting older and you're starting to look it?).

This kind of fear works. And now more than ever, companies realize it.

What's more, branding as we know it is just beginning. Expect anything and everything to be branded in the future— because as our brain-scan study has shown, our brains are hardwired to bestow upon brands an almost religious significance and as a result we forge immutable brand loyalties.

Take fish, for example.

Twenty miles off the Japanese island of Kyushu sits Japan's Bungo Channel, where the waters of the Pacific Ocean converge with the Seto Inland Sea. Here's where the hunt begins for a small, grayish-pink mackerel known as the *Seki saba*. Until the late 1980s, fishermen regarded *Seki saba* as a meal fit only for the poor. It was plentiful, cheap, and it went bad overnight. Until 1987, *Seki saba* yielded merely 1,000 yen apiece—around ten dollars—and its low rate of return left many fishermen with little to show for a day's work but the mackerel itself.

But in 1988, something happened that shook up and re-drew the rules of Japan's local and national mackerel market: over the course of that year, the retail price for *Seki saba* sky-rocketed by approximately 600 percent. So how had an unexceptional fish become one of the hottest things in Japan practically overnight?

By becoming a brand. In 1998 the Japanese government awarded *Seki saba* an official certificate attesting to the fish's superior taste and high quality. And this stamp alone was enough to transform popular perception—in a country of approximately 125 million people—to such a degree that it could justify a 600 percent price increase. "We knew if we could differentiate, we could charge a higher price," confirmed Kishichiro Okamoto, who heads the Saganoseki branch of the Oita Prefecture fishermen's cooperative. First, Okamoto branded the *Seki* name, linking the mackerel with the Saganoseki region in which it could be found. Then he drew up a set of rules dictating which fish could be considered authentic *Seki saba* and which could not. Under the new rules, only *saba* caught with rods qualified as *Seki saba,* as fish caught with traditional nets were considered too bruised and damaged. According to Okamoto, *Seki saba* must also be killed by a local technique known as *ikejime* that involves puncturing holes near the gills and tail to drain the fish's blood cleanly and efficiently. And in order to bypass excessive handling, *Seki saba* was not to be weighed or measured. Instead, wholesale purchasers had to engage in "face buying" and select their *Seki saba* just by giving the fish a thorough visual once-over.

By the time I left the Tokyo fish market at dawn one cold September morning, nothing was left of the *Seki saba* displays but empty boxes. It didn't matter that *Seki saba* looked exactly like *Seki isaki* and *Seki aji,* its fishy brethren. Japanese fish buyers had to have the *Seki saba* brand.

Every one of us ascribes greater value to things we perceive—rationally or not—to be in some way special. Let's say you're turning forty today, and in honor of your birthday, I hand you a beautifully wrapped box. Undoing the paper, you remove a small gray rock. Dull, average, ugly, the sort of rock you might see lying on the side of road. "Thanks a lot," you're thinking.

But what if I proceed to tell you that this isn't just *any* rock you're holding, but a one-of-a-kind rock, a historical symbol, a fragment of the Berlin Wall that was smuggled out of the country days after the wall's destruction in 1989, when East and West Berliners began snatching up chips and chunks of the fallen barrier as keepsakes. You now have in your possession a talisman symbolizing the end of the cold war.

"Thanks a lot," you say, this time meaning it.

"Anytime," I answer. "Here's to turning forty." A moment goes by. Then I tell you I was just kidding. The rock doesn't come from the Berlin Wall—it's even more exceptional than that. The rock you have in your hand is an authentic moon rock, a chunk of the roughly six ounces of lunar detritus that Neil Armstrong and his fellow astronauts brought back home with them during their 1969 Apollo 11 mission.

A moon rock is pretty special. There are a limited number

of them in the world. And after all, it comes from the moon. What an exquisite present, you think. You're shocked, genuinely overcome.

The fact of the matter is that I found the rock by the side of the road, put it in my pocket, and threw it into a box. Aside from the everyday miracle of geology and tectonic plates and all that, it's just a rock. But once I stamped it with certain properties—historical significance, geological rarity, whatever—it became so much more. In other words, when we brand things, our brains perceive them as more special and valuable than they actually are.

Another thing I believe we'll be soon seeing is the advent of the twenty-four-hour human brand. Take Paris Hilton, for example. Many of us have little respect for her, but the fact remains she's become a walking, talking, giggling, partying brand. Whether she's starring in an amateur Internet porn film, dancing at a new Tokyo nightclub, promoting her new clothing line, or doing a stint in jail, Paris is a human brand that creates headlines and publicity wherever she goes. Similarly, the larger-than-life CEO of Virgin Atlantic, Richard Branson, has become less a business tycoon than a living brand. Whether he's spending the week at his private Caribbean island, hot-air ballooning over France, or announcing plans to rocket to the moon, he's never far from the public eye. And in the future, I think companies will embrace personal brands more and more, creating real characters in order to get more exposure, and in turn sell more stuff.

But this is all just the beginning.

My study has, I hope, helped to demystify much of what goes on in our subconscious minds. And that has far broader implications than helping some guy in an office think up new ways to convince consumers that his tap water was actually bottled by the von Trapp children during an Alpine bike ride.

Neuromarketing is still in its infancy, and in the years ahead, I believe it is only going to expand its reach. Though it may never be able to tell us *exactly* where the "buy button" resides in our brains—*and thank God for that,* a lot of people may say—it will certainly help predict certain directions and trends that will alter the face, and the fate, of commerce across the world.

And anyway, what choice do we have? Can we, as individuals, escape the reach of marketers and brands and the new face of advertising that appeals to our subconscious minds? It's not easy to do in today's world. Perhaps, if you drove to the supermarket, loaded up on food for the next decade or two, and then locked yourself inside your house or apartment with double-bolts. Unplugged your television. Switched off your cell phone. Canceled your high-speed Internet connection. In other words, cut yourself off from the outside world altogether.

But I suspect life would get a little stale and dull before long. You would be safe from marketers, but at what cost?

The alternative? A world in which you face the onslaught of advertising with a better understanding of what drives and motivates you, what attracts and repels you, what gets under your skin. A world in which you are not a slave to the mysterious workings of your subconscious, nor a puppet of the marketers and companies that seek to control it. A world in which before rushing out to buy that new vanilla-scented skin cream or that shampoo with the mysterious X-factor or that pack of Marlboros that your rational mind knows will deposit fat globules into your lungs, you will pause. Because that is a world in which we, the consumers, can escape all the tricks and traps that companies use to seduce us to their products and get us to buy and take back our rational minds. And I hope that by writing *Buyology*, this is the world I have helped bring about.

So be mindful.

P.S.: If you want to continue this journey into your Buyology, log on to www.MartinLindstrom.com and step into a world—with its truths and lies—which we've just begun to understand.

Most research experiments on the scale of those that make up *Buyology* involve months, if not years, of planning, discussion, and evaluation. Typically, a researcher comes up with a hypothesis, researches it, refines it, then designs a model to test it, all before finally proceeding to the actual experiment.

The studies that underlie *Buyology* were no different. I began with a number of hypotheses, all based on what I'd learned and observed in my two decades of helping companies build lasting brands. One hypothesis was that cigarette warning disclaimers actually encouraged smoking. Another was that product placement is largely useless. Yet another was that there exists a strong alliance between brands and ritual and religion. Then I took these hypotheses, and after doing the necessary research, thought up a way to test them, using cutting-edge neuroimaging techniques.

But of course, I lacked both the equipment and the scientific background to do this alone. That's why I enlisted the help of two top researchers, Dr. Gemma Calvert and Professor Richard Silberstein.

Dr. Calvert, who holds a Chair in Applied Neuroimaging and is Director of the new fMRI Centre at the Warwick Manufacturing Group,

University of Warwick, and co-founder of Neurosense in Oxford, spear-headed our fMRI experiments. FMRI (Functional Magnetic Resonance Imaging) scanning is a safe, non-invasive technique that records and measures brain activity associated with perception, cognition, and behavior. When a task is performed, the neurons involved in the task become active, or "fire," emitting electrical impulses. Energy in the form of oxygenated blood (a magnetic substance produced from the iron in blood) then flows to these active brain areas, changing the magnetic properties of these regions by tiny but measurable degrees. Using a large magnet (about 40,000 times greater than the earth's magnetic field), fMRI measures these changes in the distribution of oxygenated blood during and after the task. With the help of sophisticated computer programs that analyze associated changes in the magnetic properties across the whole brain, Dr. Calvert and her team are able to pinpoint and quantify changes in brain activity in response to various stimuli with extraordinary spatial resolution (i.e., within one to two mm.) Though not without its critics, fMRI is generally considered to be one of the most accurate and reliable brain imaging tools available today.

With a staff of four full-time researchers and five part-time staff, Professor Richard Silberstein, who holds a Chair of Cognitive Neuro-science and is the CEO of Neuro-Insight, conducted the Steady State Topography (SST) portions of our experiment. SST, which Professor Silberstein developed, is a technique that uses a series of sensors to measure minute electrical signals in a dozen discrete areas of the human brain (the posterior parietal cortex, anterior cingulate gyrus, prefrontal cortex, basal forebrain, mediodorsal nucleus, amygdala, hippocampus, inferotemporal cortex, right prefrontal cortex, right parietotemporal cortex, and orbito-frontal cortex). Because the brain is specialized, with specific physical regions clearly associated with specific cognitive functions, SST offers clues as to what cognitive functions (arousal, engagement, etc.) are taking place in response to various stimuli. Because it measures these electrical signals up to thirteen times per second, SST, unlike fMRI, provides what amounts to a real-time activity log for those dozen brain regions.

Each one of the fMRI experiments in *Buyology* was approved by the Central Ethics Committee in the United Kingdom. First we submitted an application describing what visual stimuli we planned to show a certain number of volunteers, as well as how we planned to recruit these volunteers (by hiring several recruitment companies). All of our petitions were approved, and our experiments were deemed to pose no risk to our volunteers. Once selected, the volunteers were fully briefed on the parameters of each experiment, and each received a per diem as a token of appreciation for their participation.

Since Neuro-Insight, the company that performed our SST scans, is an independent market research service provider that uses its own brain measurement equipment and resources, and accordingly does not need to access any university facilities, it was not subject to the same ethical review proceedings as the fMRI experiments. However, Neuro-Insight conforms to the national or international legislation that applies in the countries in which the company operates, and follows established market research industry codes of practice in those countries—meaning that Neuro-Insight informs volunteers clearly, fully, and honestly about its techniques and obtains their explicit written consent to take part. Once a study begins, the participants can terminate their involvement in the study at any stage; however, none of the participants in our *Buyology* experiments chose to do so.

ACKNOWLEDGMENTS

A few years back, some friends and I embarked on the Harbour Bridge Climb in the middle of Sydney Harbour in Australia. It's a four-hour-long ascent that takes you along catwalks and corridors and ladders until at last you reach the summit of the Sydney Harbour Bridge. The view is, of course, spectacular. You can see every building, every rooftop, every passing ship. I rarely do things like this—it's a little touristy—but I won't ever forget that afternoon. It wasn't because I'd never seen the city from that height (because I do, every time I fly in from one of my never-ending journeys), it was because of our guide. His name was Adam, and he was inspiring.

Once we reached the top of the summit, I asked him: How did he manage to stay so motivated and engaged, despite having seen and done this so many times before? What was his secret? How could he keep from yawning, tuning out, just going through the motions?

Adam informed me that every member of the Sydney Harbour Bridge Climb team has to go through a four-month-long training program. The first month they're trained in storytelling—in conveying interesting messages to all kinds of people from every background and culture. They also learn to memorize people's names, which they manage to do in less than two minutes. The second month they're taught how to deal with climbers' panic attacks. After all, the top of the bridge is a long way up from the water, the staircases are cramped, the corridors are narrow, and if you're a person at all prone to anxiety, well, this is hyperventilation-central.

I broke in: "And then you spend the last two months of your training learning about the history of Sydney and the Harbour Bridge, right?" No, Adam replied. Instead, guides-in-training are asked to spend the third month conducting their own research, talking with people who work, or have worked, on the seventy-five-year-old bridge, including painters, mechanics, and even the relatives of people who were involved in building the bridge. Why? So that instead of just learning to recite and repeat tired sound bytes, the guides can come up with their own stories. "That's the reason why I'm so motivated," Adam told me. It was why he never got tired of doing what he did: The stories were his own.

Three years after I embarked on this journey, that's the same reason why I'm still so excited about discovering our Buyology. It's my own venture into uncharted territories, one that no one has ever explored before to this degree. But just as it took thousands of people to construct the Harbour Bridge (including a few casualties), carrying out this amazing study, raising the money, and finally writing this book required a truly remarkable team.

Peter Smith converted my voice, my thoughts, my rusty writing, my bad jokes, and Dinglish (a combination of Danish and English) into American. But not only that, he did it in the most amazing and fun way. He's the type of guy who everyone falls in love with—my PA (personal assistant) in Europe, my PA in Asia, my project managers, everyone! He's a master of fine writing, taking a sophisticated scientific project into an easy-to-read and enjoyable narrative. Well done, Peter—you're my absolute hero. With Peter comes his friend—and my friend—Paco Underhill. It's like we're all one big family, you see? Paco, thank you so much for everything. From the very beginning you've pushed me, inspired me, and prodded me to get to this point. You, and your wonderful, talented partner-in-life, Sheryl Henze, are true friends.

My agent, James Levine, together with my favorite editor, Roger Scholl, glimpsed the vision behind this book long before I did. I was about to begin writing yet another boring business-to-business book when they held up their hands and said *Stop! This book isn't just for business-people, it's for everyone.* They were right. Roger, you've been fantastic to work with. Thank you for always being there and for crafting the angle of this book into what it is today. Jim, thanks for believing in this project when no one else did—I still remember our walk in subzero temperatures along the sidewalks of New York from one publisher's office to another when you turned to me and said, "I can feel there's something in the air." It gave me chills, in more ways than one. Thanks go as well to everyone else at Levine/Greenberg Literary Agency, including Lindsay Edgecombe, Elizabeth Fisher, Melissa Rowland, and Sasha Raskin.

The work really begins when your work comes back covered in more red ink than black. Talia Krohn—I salute you, and bravo. You've been the never-ending critical voice asking all those questions we secretly hoped wouldn't occur to you, but did anyway. Thank you so much for all your hard work and incredible efforts. I can picture you at your desk, buried under thousands of pages with your awful little red pen. (Please, please, won't you change the color to blue next time? The red color reminds me of school.) Thanks to you and Roger we've ended up with what I think is an amazing piece of work.

Then there's everyone at Random House and Doubleday: Michael Palgon, the deputy publisher of Doubleday, who has always been a staunch supporter and advocate; Meredith McGinnis and Emily Boehm in marketing; Elizabeth Hazelton and Nicole Dewey in publicity; and Louise Quayle in sub rights for your remarkable work in crafting a package around my book which the world loved. Jean McCall, Ceneta Lee-Williams, Amy Zenn, and the rest of the hardworking and extraordinary sales team began spreading the word-of-mouth on this book early on and continue to this day.

To be honest, my fear that science and marketing would clash proved to be unfounded. The scientific team behind this book is, without doubt, the very foundation of our efforts, and it's been a joy working with every one of them. First, an enormous debt of gratitude to Gemma Calvert, Michael Brammer, and the entire team at Neurosense—I've enjoyed every minute of our partnership. I apologize for being so demanding, for asking so many dumb questions, and for interrogating you with requests, angles, and silly ideas. You always responded with good humor, which, considering the pressure I put you under, still amazes me.

Thanks go as well to Professor Richard Silberstein, Geoffery Nield, and the rest of the team from Neuro-Insight. Geoffery has inspected more brains across the world than anyone I've ever met and did an extraordinary job investigating my vision and uncovering dimensions that I'd never considered.

Another group of people deserves a very special acknowledgment—those thousands of volunteers who wage a daily fight against cigarette smoking. I would particularly like to thank Katie Kemper at Tobacco Free Kids. Katie has done a tremendous job in spreading *Buyology*'s insights within the antismoking community. I'd also like to salute the American Legacy Foundation, the National Cancer Institute, the Pan American Health Organization, the National Institute on Drug Abuse, Pinney Associates, the Schroeder Institute for Tobacco Research and Policy Studies, and the American Cancer Society. I've sincerely enjoyed working with all of you to convert the insights from the Buyology study into solutions that will help counteract the powerful campaigns of big tobacco companies.

A special thanks to Frank Foster, a cornerstone in making BUYOLOGY INC. become a reality—and to SP Hinduja and his unique family, who have inspired some of the insights in this book.

Many people at the LINDSTROM Company and our affiliated companies (including our new, New York City–based neuromarketing company, BUYOLOGY INC.) have been instrumental in transforming this book into a reality, and never stopped pushing *Buyology* even further, especially Lynn Segal, who crafted the outline of the book; and Signe Jonasson, who, by steering me on the most complex itineraries across the world, helped bring this book to life; John Phillips and Simon Harrop from our sister company, the BRAND sense agency, for their valuable input on our senses; Julie Anixter and Duncan Berry for their in-depth insight on the topic of cognitive dimensions; and Donna Sturgess, whose personality, energy, and contributions were, and are, a constant source of inspiration.

Okay, here comes the sponsorship bit (duck!). Without millions of dollars of financial support from some of the most respected companies in the world, the pages in this book would have been, well, blank. GlaxoSmithKline (one of the leading pharmaceutical companies wordwide in providing products and solutions to help people quit smoking), Fremantle, and Bertelsmann—thank you all. Immanuel Heindrich: Who would have thought that the same project we discussed some four years ago would end up being published by a subsidiary in your group? Talk about a coincidence. Thanks, Immanuel—you're amazing.

Hakuhodo—my favorite Japanese advertising agency, which, from day one, jumped on this project. Firmenich—the world's undisputed leader in flavor and fragrances and, ever since the publication of *BRAND sense,* a big believer in what I do. CEO Tim Clegg and Americhip—a leading manufacturer in incorporating the human senses into memorable print advertising—my deepest gratitude. Firmenich and

Americhip have both put enormous effort into the release of this book, which I won't soon forget. And an enormous thank-you to the many other sponsors who were there, always, to support me behind the scenes.

But most importantly, an enormous debt of gratitude to the thousands of people across the globe who volunteered to join me on this mission. Just imagine letting someone inspect your brain in the name of exploring the future. Thanks go as well to the hundreds of project managers, coordinators, and controllers who oversaw this project, as well as to the ethical panels who oversaw and approved every single step we took.

In the end, *Buyology* isn't just my story. It belongs to everyone with a brain who wants to know the science behind why we buy and, most of all, who we are as human beings.

I feel like I'm at an Academy Awards ceremony—where's the statue?

INTRODUCTION

1. http://www.commercialalert.org/issues/culture/neuromarketing/
   commercial-alert-asks-senate-commerce-committee-to-investigate-
   neuromarketing; http://www.organicconsumers.org/corp/neuro
   marketing.cfm

1. A RUSH OF BLOOD TO THE HEAD

1. http://library.thinkquest.org/17360/text/tx-e-pod.html
2. http://www.theglobeandmail.com/servlet/Page/document/v5/
   content/subscribe?user_URL=http://www.theglobeandmail.com
   %2Fservlet%%2Fstory%2FLAC.20050611.CHINA1
3. http://news.bbc.co.uk/2/hi/3758707.stm
4. http://www.lungusa.org/site/pp.asp?c=dvLUK9O0E&b=39853
5. http://online.wsj.com/article/SB120156034185223519-email.html
6. http://www.forbes.com/forbes/2003/0901/062.html
7. http://www.allbusiness.com/retail-trade/food-stores/4212057–1
   .html

8. http://www.ixpg.com/brand-creation.html

9. http://www.smeal.psu.edu/cscr/sponsor/documents/ascn.pdf/download

10. Malcolm Gladwell, *Blink* (New York: BackBay Books/Little Brown, 2005), pp. 158–59.

11. http://www.sciencedirect.com/science?_ob=ArticleURL&_udi=B6WSS-4DJ38WF-N&_user=10&_coverDate=10%2F14%2F2004&_rdoc=1&_fmt=&_orig=search&_sort=d&view=c&_acct=C000050221&_version=1&_urlVersion=0&_userid=10&md5=97a7ba3fc02af8aca137edd9173d8cdb

12. http://www.newyorker.com/archive/2006/09/18/060918fa_fact

13. http://www.iht.com/articles/2006/02/01/bloomberg/bxbrain.php

14. http://neuromarketing.blogs.com/neuromarketing/2006/07/emotions_vs_log.html

15. J. Tierney, "Using M.R.I.s to See Politics on the Brain," *New York Times,* April 20, 2004.

16. "The Ideas Interview: Steve Quartz," *U.K. Guardian,* June 20, 2006.

17. M. Talbot, "Duped," *The New Yorker,* July 2, 2007.

18. http://miniusa.com/?#/learn/FACTS_FEATURES_SPECS/Top_Features-m

19. A. Cunningham, "Baby in the Brain," *Scientific American,* April/May, 2008.

20. J. Rosen, "The Brain on the Stand," *New York Times Magazine,* March 11, 2007.

2. THIS MUST BE THE PLACE

1. http://publications.mediapost.com/index.cfm?fuseaction=Articles.san&s=65395&Nid=33058&p=222600

2. http://publications.mediapost.com/index.cfm?fuseaction=Articles.showArticleHomePage&art_aid=57272

3. http://www.realityblurred.com/realitytv/archives/american_idol_5/2006_Feb_22_cingular_text_votes

4. http://www.mobiledia.com/news/45332.html

5. http://media.ford.com/article_display.cfm?article_id=26074

6. B. Carter, "NBC to Offer Downloads of Its Shows," *New York Times,* September 20, 2007.

7. http://www.jsonline.com/story/index.aspx?id=305598

8. http://www.nytimes.com/2007/09/20/business/media/20nbc.html?em&ex=1190433600&en=d6b6c1a881c3ccc1&ei=5087%0A

9. http://bgcooper.com/2007/05/07/casino-royale-product-placement-overload/

10. http://www.commercialalert.org/issues/culture/product-placement/plot-line-drink-pepsi

11. http://www.usatoday.com/money/advertising/2006–10–10-ad-nauseum-usat_x.htm

3. I'LL HAVE WHAT SHE'S HAVING

1. http://www.newsweek.com/id/54529

2. http://daviddobbs.net/page2/page4/mirrorneurons.html

3. http://www.nytimes.com/2006/01/24/science/24side.html

4. http://www.scenta.co.uk/scenta/news.cfm?cit_id=1140773&FAAreal=widgets.content_view_1

5. http://www.scenta.co.uk/scenta/news.cfm?cit_id=1140773&FAAreal=widgets.content_view_1

6. http://swoba.hhs.se/hastba/papers/hastba2003_007.pdf

7. K. Leitzell, "Just a Smile," *Scientific American*, April/May, 2008.

8. http://swoba.hhs.se/hastba/papers/hastba2003_007.pdf

9. C. Witchalls, "Pushing the Buy Button," *Newsweek,* March 22, 2004.

10. http://www.kansan.com/stories/2007/apr/26/serial_shoppers/?jayplay

11. http://neuromarketing.blogs.com/neuromarketing/2006/07/emotions _vs_log.html

4. I CAN'T SEE CLEARLY NOW

1. http://www.straightdope.com/classics/al_187.html
2. http://www.snopes.com/business/hidden/popcorn.asp
3. http://news.zdnet.com/2100–9595_22–517154.html
4. http://www.imbd.com/title/tt0070047/trivia
5. L. Rohter, "2 Families Sue Heavy-Metal Band as Having Driven Sons to Suicide," *New York Times,* July 17, 1990.
6. http://www.snopes.com/business/hidden/coolcans.asp
7. http://www.msnbc.msn.com/id11628155/
8. D. Westin, *The Political Brain* (New York: Public Affairs, 2007), p. 58.
9. http://news.bbc.co.uk/2/hi/in_depth/americas/2000/us_elections/ election_news/923335.stm
10. http://www.neurosciencemarketing.com/blog/articles/smiles-boost-sales.htm#more-229
11. http://wwwobserver.guardian.co.uk_news/story/0,6903,1577892 .00.html
12. http://www.nascar.com/guides/about/nascar/

5. DO YOU BELIEVE IN MAGIC?

1. http://www.esquire.com/the-side/opinion/guinness031207
2. http://www.dailymail.co.uk/pages/live/articles/technology/technology .html?in_article_id=452046&in_page_id=1965
3. Benedict Carey, "Do You Believe in Magic?" *New York Times,* January 23, 2007. http://www.nytimes.com/2007/01/23/health/psychology/ 23magic.html?ex=1327208400en=40bd663a129bebc9ei=5088partner =rssnytemc=rss&adxnnl=1&adxnnlx=1191856112–6NnqQV1z +uD/j5C57Mt/Zw

4. http://www.nytimes.com/2007/01/23/health/psychology/23magic
.html?pagewanted=2&ex=1327208400en=40bd663a129bebc9ei
=5088partner=rssnytemc=rss&adxnn1x=1191780070-Fs2ipYO
JuaesEqBsgKZYeQ
5. http://www.timesonline.co.uk/tol/news/world/article627877.ece
6. http://www.query.nytimes.com/gst/fullpage.html?sec=health&res
=9F01E4DF1F3BF933A25751C1A9649C8B63
7. http://www.aef.com/on_campus/classroom/research/data/7000
8. http://www.washingtonpost.com/wpdyn/content/article/2005/05/
11/AR2005051101772.html
9. http://www.Iht.com/articles/ap/2007/02/21/europe/EU-GEN-
Belgium-Airline-Superstition.php
10. http://www.usatoday.com/travel/columnist/grossman/2005–10–
31-grossman.x.htm
11. http://www.ottawasun.com/News/ChronicPain/2006/10/12/
2007508-sun.html
12. J. Yardley, "First Comes the Car, Then the $10,000 License Plate,"
New York Times, July 5, 2006.
13. http://www.gotmilk.com/news/news_008.html
14. http://wheresthesausage.typepad.com/my_weblog/product_rituals/
index.html
15. http://archive.salon.com/mwt/sust/2001/02/27/mallomars/print
.html
16. http://www.wtopnews.com/index.php?sid=142203&nid=25

6. I SAY A LITTLE PRAYER

1. http://www.sciencedaily.com/releases/2006/08/060830075718.htm
2. http://www.newsweek.com/id/74380
3. http://www.thedaily.washington.edu/article/2007/2/1/sundays
UpcomingPilgrimage

4. http://www.telegraph.co.uk/news/main.jhtml?xml=/news/2008/
   02/07/wpope107.xml

7. WHY DID I CHOOSE YOU?

1. http://www.iep.utm.edu/t/theatetu.htm
2. The Hidden Power of Advertising (Admap Monographs); http://
   www.amazon.com/gp/reader/1841160938/ref=sib_dp_pt/104–
   2562080–4989511#reader-link
3. http://www.willitblend.com/videos.aspx?type=unsafe&video
   =iphone□
4. http://www.youtube.com/watch?v=WI9J7MoBZbY

8. A SENSE OF WONDER

1. http://www.getrichslowly.org/blog/2007/10/02/the-smell-of-
   money/
2. http://www.nytimes.com/2007/09/09/realestate/keymagazine/
   909SCENTtxt.html?_r=2&ref=keymagazine&pagewanted=print
   &oref=slogin&oref=slogin
3. Ibid.
4. http://scienceblogs.com/cognitivedaily/2006/09/smells_like_clean
   _spirit.php#more
5. http://news.cincypost.com/apps/pbcs.dll/article?AID=/20071123/
   BIZ/711230312/1001
6. http://money.cnn.com/magazines/business2_archive/2007/04/01/
   8403354/index.htm
7. http://www.time.com/time/magazine/article/0,9171,1666274,00
   .html
8. http://www.businessweek.com/magazine/content/07_33/b4046054
   .htm?chan=search

9. http://www.freenewmexican.com/artsfeatures/10701.html

10. http://www.le.ac.uk/psychology/acn5/nature/html

11. http://www.nytimes.com/2007/12/09/nyregion/thecity/09/light .html?_r=1&oref=slogin

12. http://www.mobilemonday.net/news/nokia-market-share-breaks-40-per-cent-threshold

13. http://findarticles.com/p/articles/mi_qn4158/is_20060327/ai _n16175901

14. http://www.nytimes.com/2005/07/10/arts/music/10ryzi.html?_r =1&oref=slogin

9. AND THE ANSWER IS . . .

1. http://www.bbc.co.uk/insideout/east/series4/clive_sinclair_spectrum _c5.shtml

2. http://www.foodprocessing.com/industrynews/2006/041/html

3. http://brandfailures.blogspot.com/2006/11/brand-idea-failures-rj-reynolds.html

4. http://brandfailures.blogspot.com/2006/11/brand-idea-failures-rj-reynolds.html

5. http://www.everything2.com/index.pl?node=E.T.

6. http://www.p2pnet.net/story/12728

10. LET'S SPEND THE NIGHT TOGETHER

1. http://inventorspot.com/articles/ads_prove_sex_sells_5576

2. http://www.adrants.com/2007/09/tom-ford-and-vulva-create-new-trend-vagin.php#more

3. Ibid.

4. http://www.americanscientist.org/template/BookReviewTypeDetail/ assetid/18958

5. http://sexinadvertising.blogspot.com/

6. http://www.economist.com/science/displaystory.cfm?story_id =8770276

7. http://store.soliscompany.com/caklplin.html

8. Ibid.

9. http://www.media-awareness.ca/english/resources/educational/ handouts/ethics/calvin_klein_case_study.cfm

10. http://www.iowastatedaily.com/mews/1999/02/26/Undefined Section/Calvin.Klein.Ads.Pulled-1085369.shtml

11. http://www.slate.com/id/2092175/

12. http://www.slate.com/id/2132600/

13. http://www.ausport.gov.au/fulltext/1999/cjsm/v3n3/erdogan &baker33.htm

14. http://www.news.ufl.edu/2006/09/05/sexyads/

15. http://www.findarticles.com/p/articles/mi_m4021/is_ISSN_0163– 4089/ai_75171022

16. http://www.cnn.com/WORLD/9712/23/gorby.pizza/

17. http://online.wsj.com/article/SB119085102463240676.html?mod =mm_hs_advertising

18. http://adweek.blogs.com/adfreak/2007/09/italys-anti-ano.html

11. CONCLUSION

1. http://sg.biz.yahoo.com/071009/68/4bqns.html

2. http://www.industryweek.com/ReadArticle.aspx?ArticleID=15191 &SectionID=2

3. http://www.medicinenet.com/script/main/art.asp?articlekey=86413

4. *Guardian Unlimited*, February 5, 2007. http://www.sport.guardian.co .uk/breakingnews/feedstory/0,,-639428,00.html

The human brain is a difficult area to navigate; hacking your way through the Amazon Basin is a cinch in comparison. Knowing as little about neuroscience as I did before I began *Buyology,* I was gratified and relieved to stumble on the work of Susan Greenfield, an Oxford University professor of pharmacology. Her lucid, extremely readable books, *The Human Brain: A Guided Tour* (London: Phoenix/Orion Books, 1998) and *Brain Story* (London: BBC Worldwide, 2000), were instrumental in helping me gain a simple understanding of a very unsimple organ. They also served to remind me, over and over again, that miraculously, human beings have "minds" that can puzzle over, speculate about, and explore in depth their own "brains" (just imagine if your foot could observe its own footness).

In addition, Rita Carter's cogent, entertaining *Mapping the Mind* (Berkeley: University of California Press, 1999) clarified the geography of the brain for me even further. *How the Mind Works* by cognitive scientist Steven Pinker (New York: W. W. Norton, 1997) is also a masterful and hugely enjoyable synthesis of brain science. I cannot recommend all four books more highly.

But there always comes a moment, after reading a book, when you want to but can't ask the author a follow-up question that's just occurred to you. Which is why my thanks go again to Dr. Gemma Calvert and Dr. Richard Silberstein and their research teams, who fielded every question I asked, no matter how naïve or dopey, with grace, intelligence, clarity, and good humor. Above all, deep thanks go to my researcher, the intrepid and tireless Bobbie7, who tracked down every query I had and responded with reams of material from all over the world, quickly, generously, and thoroughly. This book couldn't have been written without her.

As I noted in Chapter 1, *Buyology* would never have taken place if I hadn't come across Melanie Wells's "In Search of the Buy Button," from a 2003 issue of *Forbes* magazine. If I'd fallen asleep during that airplane flight, or been immersed in a murder mystery, it's more than probable that the research experiments I've written about in this book would have never happened. The article compelled me to try on a new pair of glasses, and I hope by reading this book that I've helped you look at brands through a similar pair. Thank you, Melanie—I bet you didn't know your piece would inspire an entire book.

"In Search of the Buy Button" also inspired me to hunt down other writings on the subject. So I'm also grateful to the always-superb John Cassidy of *The New Yorker,* who explored neuro-economics and the brain in his September 18, 2006, article, "Mind Games" (available online at http://www.newyorker.com/archive/2006/09/18/060918fa_fact); Malcolm Gladwell, whose feverishly entertaining *Blink* (Boston: Little, Brown, 2005), a book that truly deserves its worldwide success, was extremely helpful in giving me another perspective on Dr. Read Montague's Pepsi-Coke neuro-marketing experiment; and the *New York Times*'s John Tierney, whose April 20, 2004, article, "Using MRIs to See Politics on the Brain" (also available online) brilliantly examined the use of brain-scanning to explore voters' brains. Margaret Talbot's "Duped" from the July 2, 2007, *New Yorker* helped illuminate the ethics and controversies of the use of neuromarketing in law enforcement, as did Jeffrey Rosen's article "The Brain on the Stand" from the March 11, 2007, *New York Times*.

In my chapter on product placement, countless Web sites were helpful in giving me a helicopter view of the saturation of this most traditional of selling techniques. In my chapter on mirror neurons, it goes without saying that I gained a tremendous amount of information from the work of Dr. Giaccomo Rizzolatti and his Parma, Italy–based research team. My information on the brain and schadenfreude (the pleasure we take in other people's misfortune) came from James Gorman's intriguing piece "This Is Your Brain on Schadenfreude," which appeared in the January 24, 2006, issue of the *New York Times*.

My chapter on subliminal advertising owes a great debt to countless Web sites and articles that explored the subliminal effects of popular music. I am grateful that, over the years, several observant souls have posted videos on YouTube exposing subliminal prods in everything from fashion ads to Disney movies (though I must say that subliminal seduction often lies in the eye of the beholder). The *New York Times* did its usual superlative job of covering the Judas Priest lawsuit trial, and Drew Westen's witty, provocative, groundbreaking book, *The Political Brain* (New York: Public Affairs, 2007), provided fascinating examples of political ads with subliminal overtones. This book is an essential and highly entertaining read that every voter should get his or her hands on before the upcoming (or, for that matter, *any*) election.

For my chapter on the prevalence of rituals across the globe, I was charmed, amused, and riveted by Tad Tuleja's *Curious Customs: The Stories Behind 296 Popular American Rituals* (New York: Stonesong Press, 1987). I am also grateful to (and continue to be astonished by) the brilliant and pioneering experiments carried out by Bruce Hood, professor of experimental psychology at the University of Bristol, U.K. Rumor has it that Dr. Hood is writing his own book; believe me when I say I will be the first in line to buy a signed copy. Benedict Carey's article on superstition and magic in the January 23, 2007, edition of the *New York Times* helped shed light on the topic of ritual in our lives, as did an enormous research project on rituals carried out by advertising giant BBDO and its estimable CEO, my friend Andrew Robertson. In 1981, the *New York Times* also provided a wonderful article, "Living with Collections," which chronicled the increasing rise of collectors (and this was years before eBay hit the scene!)

Hello Kitty as a cultural phenomenon has always fascinated me. Ken Belson's and Brian Bremmer's *Hello Kitty: The Remarkable Story of Sanrio and the Billion Dollar Feline Phenomenon* (Singapore: John Wiley & Sons, 2004) is the ultimate Baedeker to and history of this mysteriously mouthless, pale-eyed creature and her global domination. For a true kick, pay a visit to http://HelloKittyHell.com, a Web site created by an exasperated if good-natured man who comes home daily to find several new Hello Kitty artifacts added to what has to be among the largest collections of Hello Kitty artifacts in the world.

In researching my chapter on religion, and particularly on the Canadian "nun study," I am indebted to *Why God Won't Go Away* by Andrew Newberg, M.D., Eugene D'Aquili, M.D., Ph.D., and Vince Rause (New York: Ballantine Books, 2001), which, as its subtitle notes, explores brain science and the biology of belief. It is a fascinating take on an eternally fascinating, not to mention extremely timely, topic.

The roots of neuromarketing can be traced back to neuroscientist Antonio Damasio's assertion more than a decade ago that human beings use the emotional parts of their brain (and not just the rational parts) when they make decisions. For my chapter on somatic markers, Damasio's works were seminal, especially *Descartes' Error: Emotion, Reason and the Human Brain* (New York: Penguin Books, 2005) and *The Feeling of What Happens: Body and Emotion in the Making of Consciousness* (New York: Harvest Books, 2000). There would be no somatic marker hypothesis without Dr. Damasio's work—he coined the term—and my debt to him and his team, especially his wife, Dr. Hannah Damasio, is incalculable. U.K.-based consultant Dr. Robert Heath has also shed revelatory light on this topic.

For my chapter on the human senses, I am grateful to the staff of one of my companies, BRAND sense agency, as well as to the executives of Firmenich for their contributions and support. In the July 10, 2005, issue of the *New York Times,* Melene Z. Ryzix wrote a fascinating piece on the enduring and ubiquitous popularity of the Nokia ring tone. In my chapter on *Quizmania,* a Web site whimsically known as Brandfailures helped focus my thoughts on a few highly anticipated products that never quite lived up to marketers' expectations.

And for my chapter on sex in advertising, I gleaned valuable insight from a Web site known simply as http://www.sexinadvertising.blogspot .com—as well as from a fascinating March 2007 article in *The Economist* called "The Big Turn Off," which explored the differences between how men and women react to ads with sexually charged content.

In my conclusion, I'm indebted to the *Guardian* for their exploration of what Super Bowl ads *really* meant to a cross-section of television viewers.

Mostly, I am, and remain, grateful to all the companies who've hired me to globetrot, visit their countries, explore their businesses, decipher their brands, and come back home with even more stories than Scheherazade. Thank you all.

MARTIN LINDSTROM is one of the world's most respected marketing gurus. With a global audience of over a million people, Lindstrom spends three hundred days on the road every year, sharing his pioneering methodologies through speaking engagements and consultancies. The CEO and chairman of the LINDSTROM Company, and chairman of the BRAND sense agency and BUYOLOGY INC., Lindstrom advises the top executives of companies including the McDonald's Corporation, Procter & Gamble, Yellow Pages, Nestlé, American Express, Microsoft, the Walt Disney Company, and GlaxoSmithKline. He has been featured in the pages of the *Financial Times, USA Today, Fortune,* the *Washington Post,* and more. A contributor to the prestigious *Contagious* magazine and *Harvard Business Review,* Lindstrom has a creative agenda that is followed enthusiastically by marketing professionals and leading academics around the world. His previous book, *BRAND sense,* was acclaimed by the *Wall Street Journal* as one of the ten best marketing books ever published. *Buyology,* like *BRAND sense* before it, has been translated into over twenty languages. Visit www.MartinLindstrom.com for more.